GRAND NOTES

THE LEGENDARY ANTIQUE DOLL
COLLECTION OF CAROLE JEAN ZVONAR

Through this book the Schoenhut piano is shown to aid the viewer in the scale of the objects. It appears as lot 254 and is 27" high.

Theriault's
the dollmasters

To order additional copies contact:

Dollmasters, PO Box 2319, Annapolis, MD 21404

Tel. 800-966-3655   Fax 410-571-9605

www.dollmasters.com

Art Direction & Design: Travis Hammond

Photography: Gerald Nelson

Production Design: Cindy Gonzalez

Conservation Department Director: Kristen Hadjoglou

Senior Conservator: Terry Lanford

$59

ISBN: 1-931503-46-X

Printed in Hong Kong

This antique doll collection auctioned by Theriault's of Annapolis, Maryland, July 15, 2007. *www.theriaults.com.*

Introduction

When Dr. Carole Jean Stoessel Zvonar tells you that she has collected dolls from the age of 5, she isn't referring to the play dolls that were popular when she was a youngster in the late 1930's. She means that she has always collected *antique* dolls. "I bought my first antique doll for $1 when I was 5 years old", she said, "Antiques are the only dolls I have ever loved".

If it is true that each person brings her own vision, consciously or not, to the congregation of dolls that becomes her collection, then the life story and circumstances of that collector are important to know. In the case of Carole Jean, it is a study of charming contradictions. What else could we expect from this diminutive

force of nature whose spirit is 19th century but whose brilliant mind is front and center of the 21st? After all, graduating valedictorian of her Salisbury High School class, all the while a brilliant pianist whose plans included a performance at Carnegie

Below: The exceptional "Riesenbaby" (literally, Giant Baby) of Kley and Hahn created only in 1912 to inaugurate their line of more standard baby dolls is an astounding 37" tall, and is surrounded by a group of German bisque characters, ladies, children, googlies, and storybook characters such as Max and Moritz.

"This 42" fellow stood in a tailor shop in Philadelphia and I imagine that tailor made uniforms for the Philadelphia fire department because that's what he is wearing. Even the buttons are marked F.D. Philadelphia. His name is George Burns because my Daddy had an uncle who was a rather dashing guy who was a fire captain in Philly and his name was George Burns. Alex gave him to me our first Christmas we were married."

"The Ichimatsu boy and girl have always been together. I got them in a small antique shop in Connecticut run by an Italian couple. This was in early 1970 and we were traveling with our Shetland Sheep mixed dog named Poulet. I spotted the dolls. I had never seen anything like them. They said they got them from a home and they had always been a pair. They seemed shocked I loved them instantly. The lady, I think, loved them some".

Hall, going on to win her medical degree at Bowman Grey School of Medicine (later re-named Wake Forest), interning at Columbian Presbyterian in New York, continuing there in research in the fields of medical pathology and medical microbiology research, Dr. Carole Jean Stoessel Zvonar gave it all up to return to Salisbury to care for her beloved mother, India, and father, Frank, and to become the wife of Alex, a calming oarsman in her whirlwind seas.

A conversation with Carole Jean is a bit like reading a Southern novel. The question you asked begins to be answered, then diverts into a different lane, turns another corner, skips back to the point, pauses, and whisks away breathlessly to

Below: A sampling of the superb automata from the Carole Jean Zvonar collection range from the uniquely sculpted Asian Tea Server to a charming "Young Girl with Sea Shell and Flute" seeking for mermaids.

still another place in her vibrant memory. The conversation is, in fact, more a chronicle of an interesting and multi-layered life where nuance matters and the details count, more than it is an answer to your simple question.

"Max and Moritz belonged to a German butcher in Philadelphia. He bought them new. They belonged to one other woman and then me. They were bought together new and have always been together".

In her own words. *"When I was 18 I headed to New York to begin studies for a performance at Carnegie Hall. But I was a bit homesick and realized it cost so much money to do the Carnegie Hall thing as it should be done ($5000 for one performance in 1956, parties and events to meet the critics, they loved things at the Russian Tea Room). I returned home. I gave many performances for schools and colleges, played on radio and TV here in North Carolina. I just did not do the Carnegie Hall thing although I have in a way regretted it. Perhaps that had a bit to do with my being homesick. I was very young...only 18 or 19. My teacher was greatly disappointed I did not do it but he was desperately poor himself. My favorite piece that I did in public? La Campanella by*

"There are three nice original dolls that belonged to a lady in Pennsylvania and were her childhood toys. One is the soldier in brown suit, another a sailor in blue suit, and a boy all in white. This lady had the BIG Schoenhut piano and the half tester brass bed. That piano is great. The size and reach of the keys is like a real piano, i.e. if a kid learned to play it, it was the same as a real piano".

"That Bébé Elite bridegroom was in a doll wedding many years ago in New Jersey. The woman paid a real tailor $45 to make his suit. I never saw the bride and I do not think the woman did either."

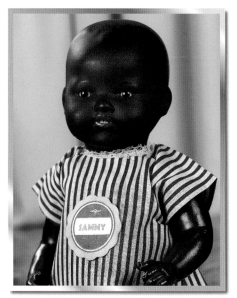

"Some of my all-original black dolls came from two nice old ladies on Howard St. in Baltimore who ran an antique shop called The Good Luck Shoppe. The dolls were old store stock from a toy store. They still have some original boxes. Have you ever seen an ethnic Hindu baby doll before? He has a turban and only one earring (made that way)."

Liszt. I played the original Liszt version, not the simplified one, one of the hardest pieces ever written for the piano. A remarkable work. I performed this at age 16 in public. Another tremendous work I did in public later as it was discovered in a library, I believe in Prague, by my own teacher, unplayed for a hundred years, was Sigismund Thalberg's Fantasy on Themes from Rossini's "Moses in Egypt."

Graduating the head of her class, Carole Jean Zvonar was one of the only women to receive a full scholarship from the Z. Smith Reynolds Foundation to study medicine at Bowman Grey School of Medicine (Wake Forest), to earn an internship at Columbian Presbyterian, then later to earn research grants where she did breakthrough studies and published papers in pathology.

Music and medicine. North Carolina and New York. Curious contradictions to which Carole Jean has been equally drawn. When she was living in one world, she was dreaming of the other. One thing tied them all together. Her love of history. Her cherishing of old things. *"I have always collected antiques. Wherever I went. Whatever else I was doing. When I went to New York City at 19 to study piano I saw 2 or 3 big dolls*

Below: Superb French bébés in the collection range from a size 16 Bébé Triste by Jumeau to a petite size 3 brown-complexioned E.J. There are a number of other beautiful Jumeau bébés including a girl in original couturier costume in the XVIIIth century style. A stunning Bru stands head and shoulders above the rest alongside a fabulous A.T. bébé by Thuillier. There is a bevy of beautiful Steiner bébés, rare Schmitt bébés including a 12" size 3/0 bébé with so-called "cup and saucer" neck attachment, and bébés by Gaultier and Joanny, among others. French poupées are well-represented including an early model wooden body Bru poupée.

"My A.T. came from a lady from up north. They retired here for warmer climate. The A.T. was named Vivian and I kept the doll's name. She bought her in Beloit, Wisconsin. She said the owners drove around with a big bisque baby in the car with them. I also bought the black E.J. from them".

"The Triste came from a collection of a woman who had every size Triste. I did not know her but a friend did. She sold them to buy a car...a Mercedes Benz, I think. I asked for the big one. If I had had lots of money I probably would have bought all of them. Alexandria Victoria was her name when I got her and I kept it".

in a store window in a Christmas scene under a big tree just like kids opening presents. It was a beautiful scene. I went inside and asked about them."

"My daddy's mother was born in Buffalo, New York, but grew up in Philly where my grandfather, William Michael Stoessel, lived. She was born in 1885 on December 22. Daddy was their first son and he was born in Philly in 1909. They moved down here [North Carolina] for a better climate in 1913. My grandmother, that I called MomMom, lived to 85 and my Granddad (Papa) lived till 91, almost 92. My Daddy remembered things about Philly all his life. We teased him about Philly because he always thought that he was Southern. On my mother's side, I am 100% Southern. Her ancestors have been here since 1725 and her dashing father was an FFV. Ancestors fought in every war...Revolutionary, War of 1812, Mexican War, Civil War (mostly Southern, but Pennsylvania cousins were Yankees), I think Spanish American War, WW1, WW2, Korean War, Vietnam and Desert Storm. My mother's own mother died when she was 46 and my mother was only 20 and I was 2. I have few vague memories of her. She was one of the most beautiful women in town. It was a tragedy. Her husband never remarried. Her daughter, my mother, is India Beatrice Aldredge Stoessel. She was named India for a Virginia cousin and Beatrice for another. I named my Bru Beatrice after my mother."

Carole Jean Zvonar credits her early interest in antiques to her paternal grandmother, Leonie Mampe Stoessel whom she called, simply, MomMom.

"Daddy's Mother became my mother's best friend, and, yes, I did grow up at her feet. She always loved old things and started selling antiques about 1938. There were a couple of other ladies around town who did the same thing. That seemed to be the way it was done...by little old ladies who picked up stuff from friends, at auction, or when somebody brought them something. They had little signs in their yards and locals knew they sold old things. She had 7 daughters and 2 sons

"The Staffordshire tea set I made poor dear Stuart take. I always liked it. Maybe somebody else will, too. It was from the collection of Jack Bordeau. He lived near or in the area called Bat Cave, N.C. up near Lake Lure and not too far from Chimney Rock. Jack was not a doll person. He collected china and glass. His place was near the Esmeraldo Inn where that man wrote Ben Hur. We met the people who owned that Inn once. I think later there was a fire...do not know what happened after".

but the one that followed her was my Mother, and, of course, me. I used to go antiquing with her and "helped" her sell in her home. MomMom liked dolls and kept a few around her, but did not collect then. She called me an old-fashioned girl. My Granddad called me Baby all my life as I was the first grandchild. So MomMom got Mother and me into antiques. They were both with me when I got my first doll.

Whether Dr. Carole Jean's interest in antiques drew her to people with similar interests, or whether her infectious enthusiasm created other collectors becomes a moot point. The chicken or the egg. Suffice it to say that where Carole Jean went, the love of things old soon followed. This love is not limited to dolls, but includes a compelling need to preserve the sense of all past things. Thus, her treasure-

"The singing birds came from Willis Stallings Antique shop in High Point, N.C. He told us it came from a local doctor's home. Willis was from an old N.C. family and knew all the old families and everyone knew him. Like me he had gone with his Grandmother when she had a shop. He was old-fashioned Southern charm. A bit of a dying kind of dignity and charm and he was quite good at really early Southern furniture".

filled historic town in Salisbury is chock-a-block with antique furniture, decorative objects, and wonderful handwind clocks that set the measure of her day with their peaceful methodical tick, tick, tick. The clocks, you see, are a special love of her husband Alex, and what led Carole Jean to her love of clockwork automata.

Carole Jean's love of all old things, in fact, so filled this home that it became necessary to have another. The Stoessel and Zvonar couples did the illogically logical thing. They bought the Queen Anne Victorian house next door, restored it to former

glory, and named it The Pink House. "I painted the house pink with white trim. There were houses that color originally in West Square [Salisbury] although this house was originally pea green and cream. But there were no pink houses left, so I did one that way." The house became an important part of Historic Salisbury tours, and soon was filled with family antiques and Carole Jean's dolls.

So involved with historic preservation of her family town was Dr. Zvonar that she served for many years on the Historical Salisbury Foundation and in 2003 she was awarded their prestigious Clement Cup given for a body of work over a long period of time over and above the call of duty. Her work continues to this day.

In her own words, from a letter of June, 2007, just last month. "It is very late tonight and I am really tired. Our Historic Foundation, especially a few 'die-hards' like me, are trying to save a wooden humpback bridge where Stoneman came into town...Sherman sent him here. We have struggled with this for 17 years and finally we may be getting somewhere. The meeting lasted three hours. My cousins came tonight from Winston and it was so good to see them. We had takeouts from the K&W cafeteria and I so seldom eat out any more that it tasted like Christmas".

It is said that stories are a part of Southern heritage. Where others are tight-lipped and emotionally still, a true Southerner is effusive and warm, unabashedly conversational. Ask her about any doll in her 400 doll collection and she'll remember when, where and why she bought it. "Oh, that great character boy in a sailor suit, he was displayed in a toy store window

Above:
Alex and Carole Jean.

of Barcelona for many years. I'm the only other person to own him", she'll say (the doll is #1 in the catalog). Her conversation continues in a delightful rapid-fire leaping from politics to pimiento cheese sandwiches to a new medical break-through for a rare disease to Lizst's Campanelli ("my favorite piano piece") until two minutes later, taking a breath for air, her eyes alight on another doll. Her friends call these The Carole Chronicles and just sit back and enjoy the ride.

A musician, yet a scientist. A preservationist, yet sensible to contemporary life. A nurturer, yet mirror clear in the expression of her opinions. Romantic, yet practical. Contradictions perhaps, but blended seamlessly in this intelligent Southern lady, allowing her to still love her dolls passionately yet giving her the strength to part with them "for their sake, so they will continue to be cared for". It is these same contradictions that blend in her superb collection, forming a perfect whole that will amaze every collector who views her tastemaker vision. ✦

1. Wonderful German Bisque Toddler, 1295, by Franz Schmidt in Rare Large Size with History

31" (79 cm.) h. 18" head circ. Bisque socket head, blue glass sleep eyes, thick dark eyeliner, painted lashes, brush-stroked brows with fly-away detail, "breather" nostrils, open mouth, accented lips, two porcelain upper teeth, tongue, brunette flocked hair, composition and wooden toddler body with chubby torso, side-hip jointed toddler legs. Condition: generally excellent, body revarnished. Marks: 1295 F.S. & Co. Germany 65. Comments: Franz Schmidt, circa 1915, the doll was displayed in the window of a Barcelona toy shop until its early acquisition by Carole Jean Zvonar. Value Points: wonderful sculpting on the rare largest size of the 1295 model, superb bisque, original toddler body, and wearing antique sailor costume and cap, leather boots, stockings, with silver whistle. $1500/1800

2. German Bisque Toddler by Franz Schmidt with Sculpted Hair

15" (38 cm.) Bisque socket head with sculpted short brown boyish hair, blue glass sleep eyes, dark painted curly lashes, rounded nose with accented nostrils, open mouth, two porcelain upper teeth, tongue, composition and wooden ball-jointed toddler body with side-hip jointing. Condition: generally excellent, hands retouched. Marks: 34. Comments: Franz Schmidt, circa 1915. Value Points: rarer model with unusual dark brown sculpted hair enhanced with decorative glaze, great antique sailor costume. $800/1000

3. German All-Bisque Googly with Swivel Head

7" (18 cm.) Bisque swivel head, large brown glass side-glancing googly sleep eyes, painted sunburst style lashes, single stroke brows, button nose with accent dots, closed mouth with watermelon slice smile, brunette mohair wig, loop-jointed bisque arms and legs, dimpled knees, painted blue socks and black one strap shoes. Condition: generally excellent, small chip at upper left leg rim, tiny pinflake on left baby finger. Marks: 189 1. Comments: Germany, circa 1915. Value Points: delightful and whimsical googly character has fine luminous bisque, well detailed dimples. $800/1000

4. Very Rare German Bisque Child, 1269, by Simon and Halbig

32" (81 cm.) Bisque socket head, brown glass sleep eyes, thick dark eyeliner, painted curly lashes, brush-stroked and feathered brows with sculpted detail, accented eye corners and nostrils, open mouth, outlined pale lips with impressed dimples at lip corners, four porcelain teeth, pierced ears, original brunette mohair wig, composition and wooden ball-jointed body, wearing lovely antique white-wear costume, undergarments, socks, shoes. Condition: generally excellent, original

body and body finish. Marks: S&H 1269 dep Germany 15. Comments: Simon and Halbig, circa 1900. Value Points: few examples of this rare dolly-face model are known to exist, having beautiful expression enhanced by large size, very choice bisque and painting. $1200/1800

5. Beautiful German Bisque Child, 1279, by Simon & Halbig with Waist-Length Original Wig

31" (79 cm.) Bisque socket head, large blue glass sleep eyes, thick dark eyeliner, painted curly lashes, brush-stroked and feathered brows with sculpting detail, shaded nostrils of upturned nose, open mouth, shaded lips, impressed dimple on center of bottom lip, and on chin, lip corners, and cheeks. pierced ears, original blonde mohair wig of extended length to the waist, composition and wooden ball-jointed body, wearing lovely antique cutwork white cotton dress, undergarments, ruffed edged bonnet, blue knit stockings, shoes. Condition: generally excellent. Marks: S&H 1279 Dep Germany 14 1/2. Comments: Simon and Halbig, circa 1900. Value Points: rare model whose fine large size allows perfect expression of the uniquely sculpted face, with generous dimples, beautiful bisque and painting, original body and body finish, rare wig. $3000/4500

6. Exceptionally Large German Bisque Child, 1248, by Simon & Halbig

37" (94 cm.) Bisque socket head, large brown glass sleep eyes, dark eyeliner, painted lashes, brush-stroked and feathered brows with modeling detail and decorative glaze, accented eye corners and nostrils, open mouth, four porcelain teeth, pierced ears, impressed dimples at lip corners and chin, original brunette mohair wig, composition and wooden ball-jointed body with pull-string "mama" crier, wearing antique white-wear dress with lace inserts, undergarments, stockings, shoes. Condition: generally excellent, original body and body finish. Marks: 1248 Germany Simon & Halbig S&H 17. Comments: Simon and Halbig, circa 1900, the model was registered in Germany in 1898. Value Points: likely the largest size of this model, the doll is enhanced by very beautiful bisque and sculpting, has rare pull-string mama crier. $1800/2400

7. German Bisque Child, "Santa" Model with Signed Santa Body

19" (48 cm.) Bisque socket head, blue glass sleep eyes, dark eyeliner, painted lashes, brushstroked and feathered brows, open mouth, outlined lips with center accent dot, four porcelain teeth, dimpled chin, pierced ears, blonde mohair wig, composition and wooden ball-jointed body. Condition: generally excellent. Marks: S&H 1249 Germany Dep 9 1/2 (head) Santa Germany (body). Comments: Simon and Halbig, their model registered as "Santa", circa 1900, the doll was commissioned from S&H for Hamburger & Co. Value Points: very pretty doll with original wig, signed Santa body, original lace and sateen dress. $900/1200

8. Very Large German Bisque Child, 1248, by Simon and Halbig

37" (94 cm.) Bisque socket head, blue glass sleep eyes, dark eyeliner and painted lashes, brush-stroked and feathered brows with sculpting detail and decorative glaze, accented eye corners and nostrils, open mouth, outlined lips, impressed dimples at lip corners and chin, pierced ears, (new) blonde human hair wig, composition and wooden ball-jointed body, antique white-wear dress and undergarments. Condition: generally excellent. Marks: 1248 Germany Simon & Halbig S&H 17 (head) Made in Germany (body). Comments: Simon & Halbig, circa 1900. Value Points: very pretty child with wide eyes, lovely bisque and painting, in largest size 17 for this model, original body with beautiful original body finish. $1800/2400

9. German All-Bisque Doll in Wedding Gown

7" (18 cm.) One piece bisque head and torso, brown glass sleep eyes, painted lashes and brows, closed mouth, brunette mohair wig, loop-jointed bisque arms and legs, painted stockings and black one-strap shoes, wearing ivory satin and lace wedding gown and veil. Marks: 203 5. Comments: Kestner, circa 1910. Value Points: pretty expression on the brown-eyed all-bisque with wedding costume. $400/600

10. Very Beautiful Early German Bisque Child, 939, by Simon and Halbig

36" (91 cm.) Bisque socket head, blue glass sleep eyes, thick dark eyeliner, painted lashes, thick dark brush stroked brows, accented nostrils and eye corners, open mouth, shaded and outlined lips, four porcelain teeth, pierced ears, brunette mohair wig, composition and wooden ball-jointed body, lovely antique cutwork white cotton dress, undergarments, stockings, shoes. Condition: generally excellent. Marks: S 17 1/2H 939. Comments: Simon and Halbig, circa 1890. Value Points: beautiful early doll with long-faced modeling, very choice bisque, original body and body finish, in fine large size that enhances the sculpting detail. $2000/3000

11. Rare German Bisque Child, 719, by Simon and Halbig with Closed Mouth

23" (58 cm.) Bisque socket head, small blue glass eyes with paperweight effect, dark eyeliner, painted lashes, thick brush-stroked brows with decorative glaze, accented eye corners and nostrils, closed mouth with primly set outlined lips, pierced ears, brunette mohair wig, early composition and wooden fully-jointed body with attached ball-joints and straight wrists, antique cashmere wool dress with silk ribbons and lace collar, lace bonnet, undergarments, shoes, stockings. Condition: generally excellent, tiny eye rim flake at inner left eye. Marks: S 13 H 719 dep. Comments: Simon and Halbig, circa 1886, the early closed mouth model was registered in that year. Value Points: rare model enhanced by most endearing expression and lovely bisque. $3000/4000

12. Superb All-Original French Bisque Bébé Jumeau in Couturier Costume and Wig

19" (48 cm.) Bisque socket head, large blue glass paperweight inset eyes, dark eyeliner, lushly painted lashes, brushstroked brows with enhancing glaze, accented nostrils and eye corners, closed mouth, shaded and accented lips, pierced ears, white mohair wig in original coiffure over cork pate, French composition and wooden fully-jointed lady body with shapely bosom, waist and derriere. Condition: generally excellent. Marks: Depose Tete Jumeau Bte SGDG 8 (head) Jumeau Medaille d'Or Paris (body). Comments: Emile Jumeau, circa 1886. Value Points: rare couturier model in virtually unplayed with condition, wearing original costume in the 18th century Marquise style decorated with silk flowers, beading, with original elaborately arranged and decorated wig, leather gloves, Jumeau undergarments, and Jumeau silk shoes with gold "Bébé Jumeau" gold lettering. $7500/9500

13. An Outstanding French Bisque Bébé A.T. , Size 10, by Thuillier

24" (61 cm.) Pressed bisque swivel head on kid-edged bisque shoulder plate, very full cheeks and lower face, blue glass paperweight inset luminous eyes of great depth, accented eye corners and nostrils, closed mouth with defined space between the shaded and outlined lips, heart-shaped upper lip, pierced ears, blonde mohair wig over cork pate, French kid bébé body with gusset-jointing at hips and knees, bisque forearms with sculpted hands and defined knuckles and nails. Condition: generally excellent. Marks: A 10 T. Comments: Andre Thuillier, circa 1880, the rarer kid-bodied model with swivel head. Value Points: outstanding quality and commanding presence of the superb French bébé with perfect bisque head, shoulder plate, and hands, each with beautifully sculpted and painted details, lovely antique lace and silk costume, bonnet, undergarments, kid shoes with silk rosettes. $40,000/60,000

14. Superb French Bisque Automaton "The Waltzing Couple" with Original Vichy Label

13" (33 cm.) Two bisque-head dolls are posed in a waltzing mode, their bodies and arms positioned as though about to twirl about, each with bisque head with portrait like features, blue glass enamel eyes, closed mouth, artfully painted lashes, brows and lips, pierced ears, the woman with bisque shoulder-plate and slender bisque arms (one sculpted bent at elbow, the other outstretched), carton upper torso and a metal cone forming her floor-length skirt and covering the clockwork mechanism; the man is attached to the lady by a hidden metal rod, each beautifully costumed in (probably original) embroidered tulle and black velvet. When keywound, the couple twirls about, pauses, glides forward and repeats the movements. Condition: generally excellent, mechanism functions well. Marks: 1 (each doll) G. Vichy Fils Paris (label on base). Comments: Gustave Vichy, circa 1870. Value Points: rare and elegant automaton with beautiful early portrait faces, wonderful movements, maker's label that is rare to find. $9000/14,000

15. Tiny French All-Bisque Mignonette

4.5" (11 cm.) Bisque swivel head on kid-edged bisque torso, cobalt blue glass enamel eyes, painted lashes and brows, closed mouth, pert smile, blonde mohair wig, peg-jointed bisque arms and legs, painted pink stockings, black two-strap heeled shoes. Condition: generally excellent. Comments: circa 1885, for the French market. Value Points: beautiful face on the tiny doll, rare pink stockings, with original chemise, "flottante" blonde wig with rose silk bows, and glass beads. $500/700

16. A French Luxury Automaton
"Lady at Her Piano" by Gustav Vichy

17" (43 cm.) seated. 16" piano length. A bisque-headed
lady with pale blue enamel eyes, painted lashes and brows,
closed mouth, pierced ears, blonde mohair wig over cork pate, carton torso, wire upper arms and
legs, carton legs in bent knee pose, metal hands, wearing elegant silk gown with black velvet ribbons,
is seated on an ebony wooden piano stool at her rosewood and ebony upright piano. When keywound,
she daintily plays the piano, flitting her fingers across the keys in a realistic manner, turning her head
side to side, occasionally nodding as though in time to the music, and now and then pausing for effect.
Condition: generally excellent. Comments: Gustav Vichy, circa 1880. Value Points: rare luxury
automata presented in luxury boutiques such as Giroux & Cie, as indicated by the fine exotic woods of
the piano ornamented with elaborate gilt ormolu and bone piano keys; the piano plays three tunes that
are listed on the original paper tune label on the reverse of the piano. $12,000/16,000

17. Beautiful and Large French Bisque Bébé Bru Jne with Wonderful Presence

28" (71 cm.) Pressed bisque swivel head on kid-edged bisque shoulder plate with modeled bosom and shoulder blades, very full lower face, blue glass paperweight inset eyes, thick dark eyeliner, painted lashes, rose blushed eye shadow, brush stroked and feathered brows, rounded nose with shaded nostrils, closed mouth with tiny stuck-out tongue, accented lips, dimpled chin, pierced ears, blonde mohair wig over cork pate, French kid bébé body with kid-over-wooden upper arms, bisque forearms and hands, gusset-jointing at hips and knees, wearing lovely antique fine white cotton dress with scalloped and cutwork edging, aqua silk sash, undergarments, leather shoes with silk rosettes signed C.M., fancy bonnet with aqua silk rosette and silk flowers. Condition: generally excellent, a nickel-sized bisque piece missing on back shoulder plate (under kid), bisque paint-skip on back shoulder plate, some body patching but overall very sturdy, perfect bisque head, arms and hands. Marks: 10 (head) Depose No.10 Bru Jne (shoulder plate). Comments: Leon Casimir Bru, from the classic era, circa 1884. Value Points: very beautiful Bébé Bru with perfectly achieved "the face", enhanced by superb bisque and painting, fine large size, perfect hands. $18,000/22,000

18. Pair of French Leather Shoes for Bru Bébé, Size 6

3" (8 cm.) Polished brown leather shoes with silver buckles, ankle straps, tan leather soles impressed "Bru Jne Paris" in oval and "6". Good condition, some overall scuffing. Circa 1885. $300/400

19. 18" French Bisque Bébé Steiner, Series C, in Size 2 with Wire Lever Eyes and Original Dress

18" (46 cm.) Bisque socket head with rounded facial shape, blue glass sleep eyes that operate from a wire lever at the back of the head, painted lashes and feathered brows, rose blushed eye shadow, accented nostrils and eye corners, closed mouth with accented

lips, pierced ears, original lambswool wig over Steiner pate (and with antique mohair wig stamped "7"), French composition fully-jointed body with straight wrists. Condition: generally excellent. Marks: Sie C 2 (impressed) (red lettered Bourqoin and Steiner stamps).Steiner (eyes). Comments: Jules Steiner, circa 1880. Value Points: very endearing expression on the little bébé with original eyes, original body and body finish, lovely antique woolen dress that appears original, straw bonnet, undergarments, stockings, leather shoes. $4500/6500

20. Very Beautiful Large French Bisque Bébé Steiner, Series C

29" (74 cm.) Bisque socket head with rounded and plump facial modeling, pale bisque, blue glass Steiner eyes that operate from wire lever at the back of the head, delicately painted lashes, brush-stroked brows, rose blushed eye shadow, accented eye corners and nostrils, closed mouth with shaded outlined lips, pierced ears, blonde mohair fleecy wig over Steiner pate, Steiner composition fully-jointed body. Condition: generally excellent. Marks: Sie C 6 (impressed on head) J. Steiner SGDG J Bourgoin (red lettering) J. St, (and cadeceus stamp on body) Steiner (eyes). Comments: Jules Steiner, circa 1880. Value Points: exceptionally beautiful large Steiner bébé with superb bisque, deeply modeled features especially around the mouth, unusual definition of ears, original wig, pate, body, body finish, fine antique costume including rare bourrelet bonnet appear original. $7500/9500

21. German Bisque Doll by Heinrich Handwerck in Wonderful Conquistador Costume

36" (91 cm.) Bisque socket head, brown glass sleep eyes, painted lashes and brows, open mouth, four porcelain teeth, brunette mohair wig, composition and wooden ball-jointed body. Condition: generally excellent. Marks: Heinrich Handwerck Simon & Halbig 8. Comments: Handwerck, circa 1910. Value Points: the very large doll is wearing a wonderful Conquistador costume that includes metal chest armor with sun shield, matching silver metal helmet with feather, fancy sword marked "Spain" with maker's name. $1100/1600

22. French Mechanical Singing Birds Attributed to Bontems

20" (51 cm.) A wooden cage with gesso sculpting and gilded finish has a gilded metal cage frame with arched top surmounted by a large brass ball and carrying handle. Inside the cage is a brass bird perch with trailing leaves and vines upon which is perched a red feathered bird; a yellow feathered bird sits nearby. When wound and lever released, the birds turn heads from side to side, flutter tail feathers, and perform a series of trills, coos, and various other authentic bird sounds. Condition: generally excellent. Comments: attributed to Bontems, circa 1880, the French automaton maker specialized in the creation of mechanical birds, a well-accomplished attempt to reconcile the French love of nature and countryside with the bustling city life of late 19th century Paris. The pair of singing birds were from the original owner home of a well-known early 20th century physician in High Point, North Carolina until their acquisition of Carole Jean and Alex Zvonar. Value Points: original and beautifully preserved mechanical birds with wonderful sounds and movements. $3000/4000

23. German Porcelain Half Doll Depicting Spanish Lady

9" (23 cm.) Waist up porcelain figure of Spanish lady having black sculpted hair with exaggerated curls, eye-shadow lined eyes, elegant slender throat, one arm at waist, the other held in front of bosom, slightly modeled away from body, and wearing elaborately draped high mantilla with sculpted flowers at waist, attached to original pin-cushion skirt base. Condition: generally excellent. Marks: 10096. Comments: Germany, circa 1915. Value Points: fine larger size with well-detailed sculpting, original pincushion. $300/400

24. Pair, Japanese Ichimatsu Dolls in Original Costumes

16" (41 cm.) Each has eggshell composition ("gofum") swivel head and limbs with painted complexion over gesso layer, enamel inset eyes, painted facial features with sculpted character details such as pierced nostrils and chin dimple, girl with black wig, boy with painted hair, each with classic Ichimatsu body with (non-working) bellows crier in mid-torso. Condition: generally excellent, original finish well preserved, some repair to original costumes. Comments: Japanese play dolls, known as Ichimatsu, late 19th/early 20th century. Value Points: wonderful character expressions on the charming boy and girl pair, each with original costumes, complexion, and well-detailed realistic boy and girl bodies. $800/1000

25. An Exceptional Luxury French Pull-toy "Moroccan with Glass-Eyed Giraffe"

24" (61 cm.) giraffe. 15' doll. 21" length. Posed upon a wooden platform with rose silk cover, gilded paper edging, and tiny spoked wheels is a bisque-headed doll with blue glass eyes, open mouth, painted features, brunette mohair wig, carton torso and legs, painted boots, wire upper arms, bisque forearms, elaborately costumed as Moroccan in silks, brocade, gold coins, and elaborate turban with beads and tassels. The doll is leading a paper mache giraffe with proudly raised head, painted flocked finish, inset glass eyes, carved mouth, with woven carpet held by leather strap. When pulled along, the doll turns its head from side to side, waves arm as though urging on the giraffe. Condition: generally excellent. Comments: French, late 19th century, a series of mechanical platform pull-toys with hidden simple mechanism under the platform were created by a firm whose name remains a mystery; the toys were presented as Etrennes in Parisian department store catalogs at that time in a variety of themes, and special commission larger examples, such as this, were created for luxury toy boutiques. Value Points: wonderful and rare pull-toy with superbly detailed antique costume and accessories, proud and well-sculpted giraffe. $6000/9000

26. An All-Original French Bisque Bébé by Steiner in Shepherdess Costume

22" (56 cm.) Bisque socket head, dark blue glass paperweight inset eyes, painted lashes, dark eyeliner, brush-stroked and feathered brows, accented eye corners and nostrils, closed mouth with defined space between the outlined shaded lips, pierced ears, white/blonde mohair wig over Steiner pate, Steiner composition fully-jointed lady body with shapely bosom, waist, and derriere. Condition: generally excellent. Marks: A -13 Paris. Comments: Steiner, circa 1890. Value Points: wonderfully preserved doll with rare lady body and original rare color wig, original body finish, lovely bisque, wearing original silk and lace couturier costume in the 18th century Shepherdess style including original gown, bonnet, undergarments, shoes and stockings. $6000/8500

27. An All-Original French Bisque Automaton "The Spanish Mandolin Player" by Lambert

20" (51 cm.) Standing upon a wooden platform with red velvet and gilded metallic cover is a bisque headed doll with brown glass eyes, mohair lashes, painted lashes and brows, open mouth, four porcelain teeth, pierced ears, brunette mohair wig, cork pate, carton torso and legs posed with right bent knee, wire upper arms, bisque forearms. Condition: generally excellent. Marks: 1300 4 1/2 S.h. dep (head) L.B. (key). Comments: Leopold Lambert, circa 1895, when keywound and lever released, music plays, the little boy moves his head from side to side, and nods, his arms move up and down as though strumming the mandolin. Value Points: an appealing parlor automaton with lovely music, is perfectly preserved, wearing magenta silk Spanish toreador costume with soutache trim, cap, and carries fine mandolin of inlay woods and mother-of-pearl. $6500/9500

28. Early French Mechanical "Lady of the Court" by Theroude in Original Costume

12" (30 cm.) A lady with paper mache head with black enamel eyes, pale complexion, open mouth with double row of teeth, original white/blonde mohair wig in late 18th century style, carton torso with lady shape, paper mache standing legs, wire upper arms, kid hands, is posed upon a three-wheeled tinplate platform. When keywound, the lady glides forward, pauses, revolves, then glides again, while her head nods and arms move up and down as though showing the flowers she holds. Condition: generally excellent. Marks: Guillard. Comments: attributed to the automaton maker, Alexander Theroude, circa 1850, and sold in the luxury Parisian toy shop, A La Galerie Vivienne, of Guillard. Value Points: very rare and superbly preserved automaton, functioning well, the lady wearing her original cream silk satin and lace fitted gown, pearls, and elaborate original coiffure with woven braids at the back of her head, with its original glass dome and wooden base. $6000/8000

29. Rare French Bisque Wooden-bodied Poupée by Bru with Original Bru Signature

14" (36 cm.) Bisque swivel head on kid-edged bisque shoulder plate, cobalt blue glass enamel eyes, dark eyeliner, delicately painted lashes and brows, accented nostrils and eye

corners, closed mouth with outlined lips and hint of smile, defined chin, ears pierced into

head, blonde mohair wig over cork pate, all wooden body with dowel-jointed articulation at shoulders, elbows and wrists, hip, knees and ankles, and ball-swivel at waist, separately carved fingers and defined toes. Condition: generally excellent. Marks: D (head and left shoulder) B. Jne et Cie (right shoulder). Modele Depose (stamp on kid collarette). Comments: Leon Casimir Bru, circa 1867, the articulated body model was deposed in 1867, based upon early artist mannequin body styles and construction. Value Points: wonderful state of preservation on the petite poupée with rare signed Bru head for this model, unusual body stamp, fine original body finish. $5500/7500

open mouth, accented lips, four porcelain teeth, dimpled chin, pierced ears, brunette mohair wig, composition and wooden ball-jointed body. Condition: generally excellent. Marks: C.M. Bergmann Simon & Halbig 13 1/2. Comments: Bergmann, circa 1915. Value Points: the doll wears its all-original WWI khaki doughboy costume with U.S. brass emblems on collar, hat, jodphur pants, boots, and his sweetheart's hankie in a pocket. The doll was from the original Becker family of Pennsylvania, along with dolls 264 and 265 of this catalog, until they were acquired by Carole Jean Zvonar for her collection. $800/1000

32. Superb German Bisque "Mein Liebling" by Kammer and Reinhardt in Original Costume

23" (58 cm.) Bisque socket head, blue glass sleep eyes, mohair lashes, painted lashes, short feathered brows, accented nostrils and eye corners, closed mouth with slightly pouty lips, brunette mohair wig, composition and wooden ball-jointed body. Condition: generally excellent, fine original body finish except retouch to hands. Marks: K*R Simon & Halbig 117 58. Comments: Kammer and Reinhardt, circa 1912, their model marketed as "Mein Liebling". Value Points: especially beautiful model with fine lustrous bisque complexion and lips, original wig and body, wonderful original white cashmere woolen sailor costume, complete set of matching undergarments, socks, leather boots, straw hat. $5500/7500

33. Large and Beautiful German Bisque "Mein Liebling" by Kammer and Reinhardt

32" (80 cm.) Bisque socket head, brown glass sleep eyes, dark eyeliner, painted dark curly lashes, short brush stroked and feathered brows, accented nostrils and eye corners, closed mouth with shaded and accented lips, dimpled chin, brunette human hair in ringlet curls, composition and wooden ball-jointed body. Condition: generally excellent. marks: K*R Simon & Halbig 117 80. Comments: Kammer and Reinhardt, circa 1912, their model marketed as "Mein Liebling" (my darling). Value Points: the largest model ever made of the desirable wistful-faced child, having finest quality bisque and sculpting, original body and body finish, beautiful antique brown wool and velvet coat and bonnet, dress, undergarments, shoes and stockings. $6000/8000

30. Exceptionally Large 42" German Bisque Doll by Simon & Halbig with Wonderful Body

42" (107 cm.) Bisque socket head with highly characterized elongated facial model, brown glass sleep eyes, lashes, painted lashes, brush-stroked brows with sculpting detail and extra feathering, accent dots at eye corners and nostrils, open mouth, accented lips, four porcelain teeth, pierced ears, brunette human hair wig, composition and wooden ball-jointed body with plump limbs. Condition: generally excellent. Marks: Simon & Halbig 9 (head) W (forehead) Heinrich Handwerck Germany 9 (body). Comments: Simon and Halbig, circa 1895. Value Points: exceptionally large child doll with beautiful bisque, original body and body finish, wonderful antique brown woolen dress with original label from Deutschmann & Birnstein of New York, undergarments, stockings, shoes. $2200/2600

31. German Bisque Child by Bergmann in Original Dough-Boy WWI Costume, from Original Owner

30" (76 cm.) Bisque socket head, blue glass sleep eyes, thick dark eyeliner, painted lashes, slightly modeled brush-stroked brows with feathered detail, accented nostrils and eye corners,

34. Exceptionally Large German Bisque Doll by Heinrich Handwerck in Superb Scottish Costume

42" (107 cm.) Bisque socket head, blue glass sleep eyes, painted lashes, brush stroked brows with sculpted modeling of brows, accented nostrils and eye corners, open mouth, shaded and accented lips, four porcelain teeth, pierced ears, brunette human hair, composition and wooden ball-jointed body. Condition: generally excellent. Marks: Germany Heinrich Handwerck Simon & Halbig 9. Comments: Handwerck, circa 1900. Value Points: exceptionally large bisque doll with fine quality of bisque, original body and body finish, wearing superb antique Scottish costume with wonderful detail including embroidered stockings, the skirt with original tailor label from "James Smart. 12 George St. Hanover Sqr London.". $2200/2600

35. German Bisque Child by Bergmann in Fine Antique Green Velvet Costume

30" (76 cm.) Bisque socket head, brown glass sleep eyes, painted lashes, brushstroked and feathered brows, accented nostrils, open mouth, shaded and accented lips, four porcelain teeth, pierced ears, antique wheat blonde human hair wig in long ringlet curls, composition and wooden ball-jointed body. Condition: generally excellent, light re-varnish of original body finish. Marks: C.M. Bergmann Simon & Halbig 13 1/2. Comments: Bergmann, circa 1915. Value Points: the pretty child has lovely bisque, and is wearing a wonderful antique costume highlighted by a green velvet coat and matching hat. $600/900

36. German Bisque Child by Heinrich Handwerck with Signed Original Body

30" (76 cm.) Bisque socket head, blue glass sleep eyes, dark eyeliner, painted dark curly lashes, incised eyeliner, brush-stroked and feathered brows, accented nostrils and eye corners, open mouth, shaded and accented lips, four porcelain teeth, pierced ears, brunette mohair wig, composition and wooden ball-jointed body. Condition: generally excellent. Marks: 109 15 1/2 Handwerck Germany 6 1/2 (head) Heinrich Handwerck Germany (body). Comments: Handwerck, circa 1910. Value Points: the pretty dolly-face model has lovely bisque, original signed body and body finish, antique costume. $600/900

37. Exceptionally Large German Bisque Doll in Philadelphia Fireman's Uniform, with Provenance

42" (107 cm.) Bisque socket head, brown glass sleep eyes, painted lashes, brush-stroked brows with sculpting detail, accented eye corners and nostrils, open mouth, shaded and accented lips, four porcelain teeth, pierced ears, brunette mohair wig, composition and wooden ball-jointed body. Condition: generally excellent. Marks: D made in Germany 20 142. Comments: Kestner, circa 1900. Value Points: largest size of this model, having fine bisque and original body finish, wearing antique blue woolen fireman's uniform with silver buttons embossed "Philadelphia F.D." along with original fireman's hat. The hat bears the emblem of Wm Horstmann Company, Philadelphia and the jacket and pants have the label of "Wm. Leopold, 6th & South St, Philadelphia". The doll was displayed in the tailor shop window of Leopold at the turn of the last century, a model for the tailor-made uniforms available from that shop, until its acquisition by Carole Jean Zvonar for her private collection. $3000/3500

Simon and Halbig, the series of Edwardian costumed ladies appeared in the 1912 catalog of SFBJ. Value Points: wonderful all-original fashionable lady, with original body and body finish, wearing original blue woolen fitted suit, lace blouse, matching wool cap, undergarments, and brown leather boots. The doll was acquired by Carole Jean Zvonar from its original Boston family owners. $1800/2500

39. Collection of Antique Purses and Accessories

6"w. largest. A collection of 11 stylish evening and beaded purses from the early 20th century, including two examples with Whiting and Davis signature, and a purse impressed "German silver". Along with two woven or faux-leather valises, and a fur stole with foxtail trim suitable for costuming larger doll. Excellent condition, the largest gold metallic with some fabric fraility on reverse side. Circa 1910. $700/1100

38. German Bisque Lady Doll, 1159, by Simon and Halbig in Original Edwardian Costume for SFBJ

18" (46 cm.) Bisque socket head with slender facial modeling, blue glass sleep eyes, mohair lashes, painted lower lashes, short feathered brows, accented nostrils and eye corners, open mouth, outlined lips, four porcelain teeth, pierced ears, brunette human hair in upswept coiffure, composition and wooden ball-jointed lady body with shapely torso, modeled bosom, waist and derriere. Condition: generally excellent. Marks: 1159 Germany Halbig S&H 6 (head) Bébé Jumeau Diplome d'Honneur (body). Comments: with original bisque head commissioned from

40. Four German Porcelain Half Dolls of Adult Ladies

4" (10 cm.) largest. Each is waist up nude figure of adult lady with arms posed expressively in various manners away from the torso, so-called "arms away", and each with variation of beautifully sculpted hair ornamented with fancy bonnet, hair band, or "jeweled" gold coronet, and painted facial features. The two smaller bear the blue stamp mark of Dressel and Kister. Excellent condition, one tiny flake on Dresden flower leaf. Germany, circa 1910. $700/900

41. Outstanding German Bisque Smiling Fashion Lady, 1388, by Simon and Halbig in Original Costume

23" (58 cm.) Bisque socket head with oval face and strong shaped chin and cheek lines, almond-shaped blue glass flirty eyes that operate from rarer glass rod inside head, mohair lashes, painted curly all-around lashes, feathered brows, accented nostrils and eye corners, closed mouth with generous smiling expression on the outlined lips, row of sculpted teeth, impressed dimples at lip corners, cheeks and chin, unpierced ears, brunette mohair wig, French composition and wooden lady body with ball-joints, and shapely torso with modeled bosom, waist and derriere. Condition: generally excellent. Marks: Bébé Jumeau Diplome d'honneur (body). Comments: Simon and Halbig's 1388 model, circa 1910; its unmarked head, French marked lady body, and original French silk costume suggest its original commissioned production for Paris boutique. Value Points: very beautiful doll with superior quality of bisque, sculpting and painting, in rare large size, has original lashes, signed body, and wears superb French silk Edwardian-era costume with plumed straw bonnet, undergarments, black stockings and leather shoes (additional silk blouse and bonnet included); few examples in this larger size are known to exist. $12,000/18,000

42. French Bisque Automaton "Little Girl with Fan and Lorgnette" by Leopold Lambert

20" (51 cm.) Standing upon a wooden platform with moss green velvet cover is a bisque-headed doll with blue glass eyes, mohair lashes, painted lower lashes and feathered brows, accented nostrils and eye corners, open mouth, accented lips, four porcelain teeth, pierced ears, carton torso and legs, wire upper arms, bisque forearms with expressively posed fingers. When wound, the doll performs a series of realistic movements, alternately turning head side to side, nodding up and down, blinking eyes, fanning herself, and then lifting lorgnette as though to peer out at some interesting scene; meanwhile music plays. Condition: generally excellent, mechanism functions well, slight fraility to original costume. Marks: 1300-6 Dep S&H. Comments: Leopold Lambert, circa 1895. Value Points: luxury parlor fancy automaton, the little girl has original fancy costume, matching fancy fan, deluxe quality gilded lorgnette, and appealing movements and music. $5500/8500

43. Extremely Rare German Bisque Fashion Lady, 1398, by Simon and Halbig, A Previously Unknown Model

17" (43 cm.) Bisque socket head portraying an adult lady with slender-shaped face having strong cheek and jaw lines, brown glass "flirty" eyes that operate from an internal glass rod, mohair lashes, painted lower lashes, daintily painted brows with light feathering, accented nostrils of elongated aquiline nose with upturned lip, virtually closed mouth with narrowest of opening below the row of sculpted teeth, impressed cheek, chin and philtrum dimples, unpierced ears, blonde mohair wig, composition and wooden ball-jointed body, blonde mohair wig, wearing antique lace dress, undergarments, rose satin boa, straw bonnet with rose silk bows. Condition: generally excellent. Marks: 1398 Germany Simon & Halbig S&H 6. Comments: Simon and Halbig, circa 1910, only one other example of the previously undocumented model is known to exist; the doll differs from its 1388 sister by slightest

mouth opening, and slightly narrower nose and firmer jawline. Value Points: extremely rare model enhanced by its compellingly beautiful appearance. $14,000/19,000

44. French Bisque Musical Automaton "The Fairy Godmother" by Roullet & Decamps in Original Presentation

20" (51 cm.) Standing upon a red velvet covered wooden platform is a bisque-headed doll with blue glass eyes, mohair lashes, painted lashes and brows, accented nostrils and eye corners, open mouth, outlined lips, four porcelain teeth, pierced ears, brunette mohair wig, carton torso and legs, wire upper arms, bisque forearms; when wound, and lever released she turns head from side to side, taps her magic wand five times, and then lifts the magic star, while music plays. Condition: generally excellent, two finger tips broken (under tassel), mechanism and music function well. Marks: 1300-6 Dep S&H. Comments: Roullet & Decamps, circa 1910. Value Points: most endearing presentation of "The Fairy Godmother", wearing her original aqua tulle and silk gown with lavish blue bead and paillettes decoration, aqua velvet slippers, gilded crown, and holding gilded magic wand in right hand and gilded magic star in left hand. $5000/7500

45. Large German Bisque Character, 126, by Kammer and Reinhardt in Bunny Costume

24" (62 cm.) Bisque socket head, brown glass sleep and "flirty" eyes, dark eyeliner, painted dark curly lashes, feathered brows, accented nostrils and eye corners, open mouth, shaded and outlined lips, two porcelain upper teeth, tongue, brunette mohair baby wig, composition ball-jointed baby body. Condition: generally excellent. Marks: K*R Simon & Halbig 126 62. Value Points: the large character baby has fine matte bisque, flirty eyes, and is wearing antique blue organdy gown with matching bunny-ears bonnet. $500/800

46. Rare German Bisque Cloth-Bodied Kewpie with Original Costume

11" (28 cm.) Bisque head with flanged neck depicting the uniquely designed Kewpie, bald pate excepting classic blonde topknot, forelock curl and above-the-ears curls, painted black side-glancing eyes, short curly lashes, dash brows, little pug nose, closed mouth with thin-line impish smile, cheek dimples, original pink muslin stitch-jointed body, bisque hands with starfish-shaped modeled fingers, sculpted blue wings. Condition: generally excellent. Marks: Made in Germany 7377 (head) 5 (arms) (frail remains of original cloth Kewpie tag on dress). Comments: Kewpie, designed by Rose O'Neill, circa 1912. Value Points: rare cloth-bodied model is all original, including original pink muslin and lace dress, has superb bisque and painting. From the original Carole Jean Stoessel Zvonar

family. Carole Jean relates "My grandmother bought each of her daughters one, purchased from the A. Parker Toy Store right here in Salisbury. One of my aunts gave me hers so I would have one in the collection. Each one had a different color dress, all pastels". $2000/2500

47. German Bisque Flirty-eyed Toddler, 2095, by Bahr and Proschild for Bruno Schmidt

20" (51 cm.) Bisque socket head, brown glass sleep and flirty eyes, dark curly lashes, short feathered brows, accented eye corners and nostrils, open mouth, outlined lips, two porcelain upper teeth, brunette human hair wig, composition and wooden ball-jointed toddler body with side-hip jointing, wearing antique cotton toddler dress with red feather-stitching, undergarments, red stockings, black shoes. Condition: generally excellent. Marks: B.P. (crossed swords) BSW (heart) 2095. Comments: Bahr and Proschild for Bruno Schmidt, circa 1915. Value Points: wonderfully expressive features, excellent bisque, endearing chubby toddler body on the rarer model. $800/1000

48. Collection of German All-Bisque Kewpies

6" (15 cm.) largest. Seven all-bisque Kewpies include two classic standing Kewpies (one with original muslin pinafore, the other with original paper label), pair of Kewpie Bride and Groom Huggers in original costumes), tiny Kewpie boutonniere with arms spread, and three tiny standing one-piece Kewpies in varying poses (each with original paper labels on back, along with a pair of Kewpie all bisque hands. Condition: generally excellent. Comments: designed by Rose O'Neill, made in Germany, circa 1915. Value Points: an appealing collection in varying sizes and poses. $600/900

49. German Bisque Character, 118, by Kammer and Reinhardt

17" (43 cm.) Bisque socket head, brown glass sleep eyes, painted lashes, brushstroked brows, accented nostrils and eye corners, open mouth with heart-shaped upper lips, two porcelain upper teeth, three impressed dimples in cheeks and chin, brunette human hair, composition bent limb baby body, antique costume. Condition: generally excellent. Marks: K*R Simon & Halbig 118 49. Comments: Kammer and Reinhardt, circa 1912. Value Points: rarer character model with distinctive sculpting of mouth and dimples, excellent quality of bisque. $700/1000

50. Wonderful German Bisque Toddler, 2072, by Bahr and Proschild

14" (36 cm.) Bisque socket head, small blue glass sleep eyes, painted lashes and short feathered brows, accented nostrils and eye corners, closed mouth with pouty expression on the downcast lips, brunette bobbed human hair wig, composition and wooden ball-jointed toddler body with side-hip jointing, antique toddler dress, undergarments, shoes and stockings. Condition: generally excellent. Marks: B.P. (crossed sword) 2072 3. Comments: Bahr and Proschild, circa 1915. Value Points: rarer model with wonderful expression, excellent bisque, toddler body with original finish. $800/1100

52. German Bisque Character, 126, by Kammer and Reinhardt with Brown Complexion

14" (36 cm.) Bisque socket head with dark brown complexion, brown glass sleep eyes, black painted lashes and brows with feathering, painted nostrils and eye corners, open mouth, coral shaded lips, two porcelain upper teeth, black mohair wig, brown composition bent limb baby body, wearing antique cotton baby dress, pinafore, ruffled bonnet, undergarments. Condition: generally excellent. Marks: K*R Simon & Halbig 126 Germany 4. Comments: Kammer and Reinhardt, circa 1920. Value Points: most appealing childish expression of delight, lovely bisque with beautiful complexion. $800/1200

53. Beautiful and Petite German Black Bisque Child by Gebruder Kuhnlenz

12" (30 cm.) Bisque socket head with ebony black complexion, brown glass sleep eyes, black painted lashes and brows, open mouth, four

51. All-Original German Bisque Nurse with Brown Complexion by Kestner for Schwarz of Philadelphia

16" (41 cm.) Bisque socket head with rich dark brown complexion, brown glass sleep eyes, painted lashes and brows, open mouth, four porcelain teeth, black mohair wig over plaster pate, brown composition and wooden ball-jointed body. Condition: generally excellent. Marks: E made in Germany 9. Comments: Kestner, circa 1900. Value Points: the doll wears her original blue chambray nursing dress with white apron and cap bearing Red Cross emblem, along with Red Cross button "I Serve", original handmade undergarments, stockings, shoes, and in (frail) original box from G.Schwarz Toy Store of Chestnut Street in Philadelphia, from the original Becker family estate of Pennsylvania. The doll has superb quality of complexion and original body finish. $1200/1800

porcelain teeth, black human hair wig, ebony black composition and wooden fully-jointed body. Condition: generally excellent. Marks: 34-20. Comments: Gebruder Kuhnlenz, circa 1890, the doll wears a lovely embroidered cotton dress with rerd silk sash, fancy silk bonnet, has original muslin chemise stamped "Kingston Jamaica" indicating her original store market, and original simple cotton print dress. Value Points: very beautiful model with well-defined features, fine quality of complexion, original body and body finish. $800/1100

53.1. Small German Brown Bisque Child Doll by Gebruder Kuhnlenz

8" (20 cm.) Bisque socket head with dark brown complexion, black glass inset eyes, painted lashes and brows, accented nostrils and eye corners, open mouth, four porcelain teeth, black fleecy mohair wig, brown composition body with jointing at shoulders and hips. Condition: generally excellent. Marks: 34-13. Comments: Gebruder Kuhnlenz, circa 1900. Value Points: lovely complexion on the little character girl, with silk dress, fancy bonnet, and with original factory muslin chemise. $500/800

54. Rare German Bisque Character "Hilda" by Kestner with Rich Brown Complexion

18" (46 cm.) Bisque socket head, small brown glass sleep eyes, black painted curly lashes, incised upper eyeliner, black feathered brows with fly-away details, accented nostrils and eye corners, open mouth, coral shaded lips, two porcelain upper teeth, tongue, black mohair wig, brown composition baby body, antique baby dress with cotton pinafore, sun bonnet with lace edging, undergarments. Condition: generally excellent. Marks: K made in Germany 14 JDK Jr. c. 1914 Hilda Ges Gesch (head) 46 (impressed on back torso). Comments: Kestner, circa 1914, their trademarked baby doll. Value Points: superior quality of bisque and richly painted complexion, original wig, plaster pate, body, body finish, on the rarely found model. $3000/4000

55. Very Rare French Bisque Bébé E.J. by Jumeau with Brown Complexion, Size 3

10" (25 cm.) Pressed bisque socket head with light brown complexion, spiral spring attachment, brown glass paperweight inset eyes, dark painted lashes, brush-stroked and feathered brows, accented nostrils, closed mouth with accented coral-shaded lips, pierced ears, black fleecy wig over cork pate, French composition and wooden fully-jointed body with straight wrists. Condition: generally excellent. Marks: Depose E. 3 J (head) Jumeau Medaille d'Or Paris (torso). Comments: Emile Jumeau, circa 1882. Value Points: rare earliest period of the brown complexioned bébé Jumeau with very beautiful complexion and eyes, original body and body finish, antique striped cotton dress, apron, undergarments, straw bonnet with black silk streamers and banding; the doll was shown in an early doll book by Janet Johl. $6000/8500

56. Gorgeous French Bisque Bébé E.J, Size 15, with Brown Eyes by Emile Jumeau

34" (86 cm.) Pressed bisque socket head with very plump cheeks, brown glass paperweight inset eyes, thick black eyeliner, painted lashes, brush-stroked and feathered brows, accented eye corners, rose blushed eye shadow, shaded nostrils, closed mouth with well-defined space between the shaded lips, separately modeled pierced ears, wheat blonde human hair wig over cork pate, French composition and wooden fully-jointed body with straight wrists, exquisite silk/woolen cream dress with tatting trim, white cotton blouse with embroidery, undergarments, lace bonnet, stockings, shoes. Condition: generally excellent, early touch-up on hands. Marks: Depose E 15 J (head) Jumeau Medaille d'Or paris (body). Comments: Emile Jumeau, circa 1884. Value Points: rare large size with superb modeling and bisque, original plump body, lovely antique costume. $8000/11,000

57. An Outstanding French Bisque Bébé Triste by Jumeau in Rare Size 16

34" (86 cm.) Pressed bisque socket head with long-faced modeling and very plump lower cheeks, brown glass paperweight inset eyes, thick dark eyeliner, painted lashes, rose blushed eye shadow, brush-stroked and feathered brows, accented eye corners and nostrils, closed mouth with defined space between the shaded and outlined lips, separately applied pierced ears, blonde mohair wig over cork pate, French composition and wooden fully-jointed body with straight wrists. Condition: generally excellent. Marks: 16 (head) Jumeau Medaille d'Or Paris (body). Comments: Emile Jumeau, his classic model known as "triste" (sad) in reference to its pouty expression, or "long-faced", sculpted by renown French 19th century sculptor Carrier-Belleuse. Value Points: the largest size made of the rare child has outstanding quality of bisque and sculpting with superb definition of expression especially around the eyes and mouth, finest painting, wearing antique multi-layered costume of fine white cotton, straw bonnet, undergarments, Jumeau socks and (frail) Jumeau shoes marked Bébé Jumeau Depose. $18,000/24,000

at forehead, painted facial features with brown eyes. Condition: generally excellent. Comments: Germany, circa 1885. Value Points: the rare-sized doll, a so-called "Frozen Charlotte", is wearing its original black knit Chimney Sweep uniform with hood and carrying a wooden handled brush. $500/700

58. German Porcelain Bathing Doll with Sculpted Blonde Hair and Pink Tinting

15" (38 cm.) One piece all-porcelain doll with pink tinted complexion overall, legs modeled apart, arms held in front of body with folded fists, sculpted short blonde curly hair with detailed locks onto the forehead, painted grey upper glancing eyes with defined threading, black and brown upper eyeliner, single stroke brows, accented nostrils and eye corners, closed mouth with accented lips. Condition: generally excellent. Comments: Germany, circa 1880. Value Points: rare overall pink tinted complexion, wonderful chubby body, detailed sculpting includes curly hair, defined ears, fingers, toes, nails, dimples. $500/800

59. German Porcelain Bathing Doll with Pink Tinting and Black Sculpted Hair

16" (41 cm.) One piece all-porcelain doll with overall pink tinting in standing pose with legs apart, arms held in front with small fists, black slightly sculpted hair with delicate stippling details onto the forehead, painted brown upper glancing eyes, red and black upper eyeliner, black single stroke brows, closed mouth, accented lips, sculpted ears, fingers, toes, dimples. Condition: generally excellent. Comments: Germany, circa 1885. Value Points: rarity factors include overall tinting, and brown eyes. $500/800

60. German All-Porcelain Bathing Doll in Chimney Sweep Costume

7" (18 cm.) One piece all-porcelain baby posed standing with legs apart and arms held in front of body with closed fists, pink tinted facial complexion, black painted hair with stippled curls

61. German Porcelain Bathing Doll in Tyrolean Costume

7.5" (19 cm.) One piece all-porcelain figure of blonde-haired child posed in classic so-called "Frozen Charlotte" pose, painted facial features, hint of smile, blue eyes, rosy cheeks. Condition: generally excellent. Comments: Germany, circa 1885. Value Points: rarer petite size, nicely sculpted hair and expression, wearing original knit costume in the Tyrolean costume with embroidery on waist sash (Fritz?). $500/700

62. Rare German Porcelain Bathing Doll with Unusual Dramatic Eye Painting

14" (36 cm.) One piece porcelain figure of young child in standing pose, legs apart, arms held in front of body with folded fists, blonde sculpted hair, painted blue eyes with large black pupils, very thick upper black eyeliner, thin line grey eyeliner above and below the eye, feathered brows, accented nostrils, closed mouth with space between the lips, pink tinted facial complexion, well defined body details of dimples, fingers, toes. Condition: generally excellent. Comments: Germany, circa 1875. Value Points: exceptional and rare "Frozen Charlotte" with unique painting of eyes lending a vivid character expression and superb modeling of hair enhanced by decorative glaze. $1000/1300

63. Very Fine German Porcelain Bathing Doll with Original Costume

14" (36 cm.) One piece all pink tinted porcelain figure of young child in standing pose with legs modeled apart, hands in loosely folded fists, shaded blonde/brown hair with brush-strokes around the forehead, painted bright blue eyes with black pupils and outline, black eyeliner, red upper eyeliner, feathered brows, closed mouth with outlined lips, unusual body mold with shapely torso, slender ankles with realistically shaped feet, defined body details of fingers, toes and dimples. Condition: generally excellent. Comments: Germany, circa 1875. Value Points: very unusual "Frozen Charlotte" model whose rarities include all-pink tinted complexion, unusual hair painting, unusual body model, very fine painting of features, and including its original costume comprising bonnet, flannel gown, undergarments. $900/1200

64. Beautiful French Bisque Bébé Jumeau, Size 16, with Outstanding "Au Bon Marche" Dress

36" (91 cm.) Bisque socket head with pale complexion, brown glass paperweight inset eyes, dark eyeliner, painted lashes and feathered brows, accented nostrils and eye corners, open mouth, shaded and accented lips, pierced ears, row of porcelain teeth, brunette human hair hand-tied wig over cork pate, French composition and wooden fully-jointed body. Condition: generally excellent, paint touch-up on torso and hands. Marks: 16. Comments: Emile Jumeau, circa 1890. Value Points: beautiful bébé with dramatic large eyes, wearing superb velvet plaid dress with original Paris label "Au Bon Marche", red velvet sash, undergarments, stockings, shoes, along with green woolen felt bonnet with original French label "Mlle Samson, Chartres", and fine antique green silk parasol. $3000/4000

65. Pretty French Bisque Bébé by Gaultier with Block Letter Markings

16" (41 cm.) Pressed bisque socket head, brown glass paperweight inset eyes, painted lashes, brush-stroked and feathered brows, accented eye corners, shaded nostrils, closed mouth with tiny modeled stuck-out tongue, pierced ears, blonde mohair wig over cork pate, French composition and wooden fully-jointed body, wearing pretty French-style brown velvet dress with burgundy trim, matching bonnet, antique undergarments, stockings, white kidskin ankle boots signed C.M. Condition: generally excellent, body is not original but is appropriately sized and of the same French era. Marks: F. 6 G. (block letters, head) Jumeau Medaille d'Or Paris (body). Comments: Gaultier, circa 1882. Value Points: very pretty plump-faced expression enhanced by lovely bisque. $3500/4500

66. A Fine and All-Original German Bisque Child by Wiesenthal, Schindel and Kallenberg

24" (61 cm.) Bisque socket head, blue glass sleep eyes, painted lashes, slightly modeled brush-stroked brows with decorative glaze, accented nostrils and eye corners, open mouth, shaded and outlined lips, four porcelain teeth, pierced ears, blonde mohair wig, composition and wooden ball-jointed body. Condition: generally excellent. Marks: S&H W.S.K. 4 1/2. Comments: Simon and Halbig for Wiesenthal, Schindel & Kallenberg of Walterhausen, circa 1900. Value Points: rarely found model in pristine unplayed with condition, original wig, body, body finish, muslin chemise with red silk ribbons, along with original undergarments (paper tags), and original red serge sailor dress and hat. $1100/1500

67. German Bisque Pouty, 7602, by Gebruder Heubach in Antique Costume

20" (51 cm.) Solid domed bisque socket head with pink tinted complexion, blonde sculpted boyish hair, intaglio blue eyes with large black pupils, white eyedots, red and black upper eyeliner, modeled "stuck-out" ears, closed mouth with downcast pouty expression, accent line between the lips, composition and wooden ball-jointed body. Condition: generally excellent. Marks: 7902 Heubach (sunburst mark) Germany. Comments: Gebruder Heubach, circa 1912. Value Points: fine quality of sculpting, bisque and painting, original body finish, fine antique blue velvet sailor costume, red knit stockings, red shoes. $700/1000

68. German Bisque Marotte with Complete Musical Tune

11" (28 cm.) A bisque head with blue glass eyes, painted features, closed mouth, blonde mohair wig, is attached to a ball-shaped body that disguises a musical mechanism, and supported by a wooden handle. The figure is costumed as a jester with metallic trimmed costume, lace collars and jester cap. When twirled, music plays. Condition: generally excellent. Comments: Germany, possibly Zinner and Sohne, circa 1890. Value Points: wearing original costume, very beautiful face, a well-detailed actual musical tune is heard rather than more commonly found musical notes. $800/1100

69. All-Original Rare German Bisque Toddler, 115 with Modeled Hair, by K*R

15" (38 cm.) Solid domed bisque socket head, sculpted light brown hair in side-swept boyish fashion with forelock, and detailed stippling enhanced by decorative glaze, brown glass sleep eyes, painted curly lashes, lightly feathered brows, accented nostrils, closed mouth with pouty expression, plump cheeks, composition and wooden ball-jointed toddler body with side-hip jointing, antique night gown and under slip. Condition: generally excellent. Marks: K*R S&H 115 38. Value Points: Kammer and Reinhardt, circa 1912, from their art character series. Value Points: rare modeled hair variation of "Phillip", 115 model, with superior quality bisque and painting, luminous quality of complexion, original body and body finish, from the home of the original owner on Eastern Shore of Maryland prior to its acquisition by Carole Jean Zvonar. $3500/4500

70. An Extraordinary German Bisque Character "Riesenbaby" by Kley and Hahn, Possibly One-of-a-Kind

37" (94 cm.) Solid domed bisque socket head, painted blonde baby hair with sculpted forelock curl, very plump face with sculpted double chin, dimples and over-sized ears, brown glass eyes, painted lashes, feathered and brush-stroked brows, accented eye corners and nostrils, closed mouth modeled as though open with defined tongue, accented lips, composition bent limb baby body, antique organdy gown. Condition: generally excellent, some slight body repair. Marks: 571 K&H (in banner). Comments: Kley and Hahn, 1912, the exceptionally large doll was made in this size only, presented in the firm's 1912 advertising (the same year that the firm introduced their line of standard size babies, see advertising on opposite page) and was likely created as a promotional exhibition doll for that year's Leipzeug Toy Fair. Kley and Hahn named the doll "Riesenbaby" (Giant Baby) in their promotions to distinguish it from the standard line. The overall length is 37", the head circumference is 37", head length is 11", the hips measure 27" above the legs or 34" including the legs. The unlikely size and the hand-sculpting details of the amazing body add credence to the likelihood that no other dolls of this model were ever made. The doll is from the ex-collection of Ralph Griffin before its acquisition by Carole Jean Zvonar. Value Points: the exceptional size of the unique doll partners with exemplary sculpted bisque and painting and its wonderful original body. Just 5 years short of its 100th birthday, the doll may be one of the rarest in the world. $12,000/18,000

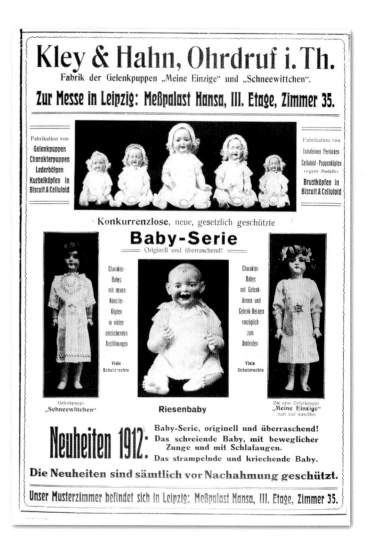

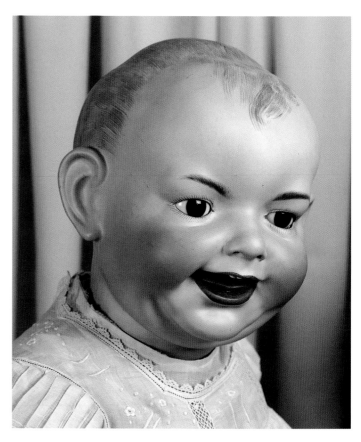

71. Beautiful German Bisque Child by Kammer and Reinhardt in Grand Size

40" (102 cm.) Bisque socket head, large blue glass sleep eyes, thick dark eyeliner, painted lashes, brush stroked brows with modeling and comb-marked details, accented eye corners and nostrils, open mouth, shaded and accented lips, four porcelain teeth, pierced ears, blonde mohair wig, composition and wooden ball-jointed body, antique whitewear dress with embroidery, undergarments, stockings, shoes. Condition: generally excellent. Marks: K*R Simon & Halbig 100. Comments: Kammer and Reinhardt, circa 1910. Value Points: exceptionally large child is enhanced with superb quality of bisque and painting, original body and body finish. $2000/2500

72. Wonderful German Bisque Toddler, "Phillip", Model 115/A, by Kammer and Reinhardt

12" (30 cm.) Bisque socket head with plump facial modeling, blue glass sleep eyes, painted short curly lashes, feathered brows, accented nostrils, closed mouth with accented lips, blonde mohair bobbed wig, composition and wooden ball-jointed toddler body with side-hip jointing. Condition: generally excellent. Marks: K*R Simon & Halbig 115/A 34. Comments: Kammer and Reinhardt from their art character series, the pouty faced model marketed as "Phillip", circa 1912. Value Points: wonderful size of the wistful faced toddler, with superb luminous bisque, original body and body finish, original cutwork dress and matching bonnet, matching two-piece undergarment set, socks, kidskin slippers. $2000/2500

73. German Bisque Character Pouty "Hans" by Kammer and Reinhardt

13" (34 cm.) Bisque socket head, painted large blue upper glancing eyes, thick black upper eyeliner, one stroke tapered brows, accented nostrils, closed mouth with very full pouty lips, accent line between the lips, blonde mohair wig, composition and wooden ball-jointed body. Condition: generally excellent. Marks: K*R 114 34. Comments: Kammer and Reinhardt, circa 1910, the model "Hans" from their art character reform series. Value Points: excellent bisque and painting on the pouty faced child, original body and body finish, antique costume. $2000/3000

74. Extremely Rare German Bisque Character, 174, by Mystery Maker

19" (48 cm.) Solid domed bisque socket head portraying a laughing child with highly characterized features, painted blonde short boyish hair, intaglio blue eyes with large black pupils and white eyedots, black and red upper eyeliner, fringed brows

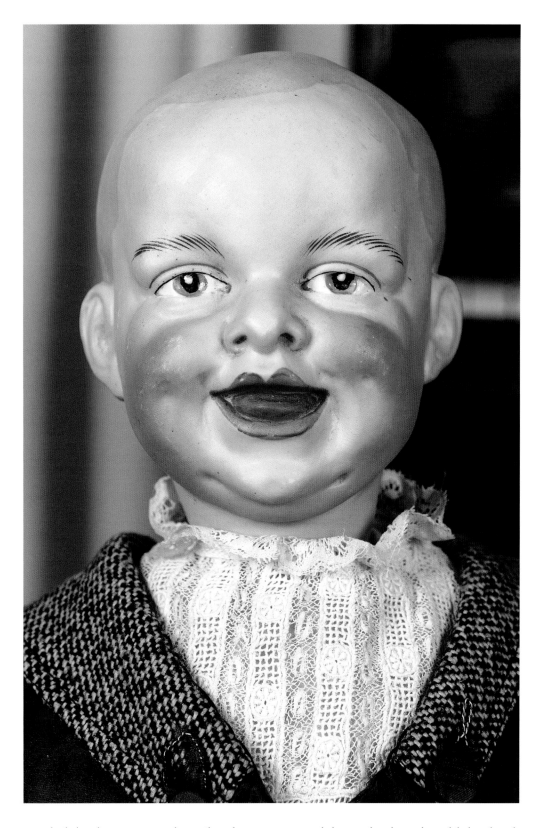

over shaded undercoat, accented nostrils and eye corners, rounded nose, closed mouth modeled as though open in laughing expression, shaded and outlined lips, modeled tongue, impressed dimples and laughter lines, composition and wooden ball-jointed body with side-hip jointing, antique woolen coat, trousers, shirt, saddle shoes, undergarments. Condition: generally excellent. Marks: 174. Comments: mystery maker, possibly Hertel and Schwab, as indicated by the style of doll, the style of the incised number, and by this missing number in their model sequence, circa 1912. Value Points: extremely rare, previously undocumented character with wonderful expression appearing almost as hand-pressed in its sculpting detail, finest quality of bisque and painting, original toddler body with original finish. $7000/10,000

75. German Wax Doll in Patriotic Costume with Provenance

14" (36 cm.) Wax over paper mache shoulder head, blue glass inset eyes, painted lashes, brows and lips of closed mouth, blonde mohair wig, muslin body, paper mache lower arms and legs, painted boots. Condition: fair, although preserved under a glass dome the wax has typical scratches and fading. Comments: circa 1865, the doll wears a unique Stars and Stripes costume of silk satin with applique paper stars, matching cap, and carries a very, very tattered American silk flag. Accompanying the doll is an issue of The Philadelphia Inquirer dated April 20, 1865, devoted to the assassination and funeral ceremonies of Abraham Lincoln. According to oral history, the doll was presented to Georgianna and Maurice Barrymore by Mary Todd Lincoln; it remained in the Barrymore family until its acquisition by Carole Jean Zvonar. Value Points: an intriguing doll with fascinating historical connections, original costume and early tattered flag, original 1865 newspaper, along with original glass dome and base. $600/900

76. Rare German Brown-Complexioned Paper Mache Boy in Original Costume

10" (25 cm.) Paper mache shoulder head with sculpted short black curly hair and dark brown painted complexion, painted facial features, closed mouth, brown muslin slender body, carved wooden brown lower arms and hands, and lower legs. Condition: generally excellent. Comments: Germany, circa 1860. Value Points: very rare paper mache doll with fine original finish, original sturdy body, and wearing original linen and homespun costume. $700/1100

77. Pair, German Brown Bisque Dolls with Sculpted Hair

11" (28 cm.) Each has bisque shoulder head with rich dark brown complexion, sculpted hair in tight black short curls, painted facial features, brown eyes, closed mouth, black sculpted brows, muslin body with brown bisque lower limbs. Condition: generally excellent. Comments: Germany, circa 1890. Value Points: excellent detail of sculpting and beautiful painting, one with antique costume and bisque bare feet, the other with rare original printed muslin body and painted grey shoes. $500/900

78. German Bisque Lady Doll with Sculpted Hair and Gold Bead Ornaments

20" (51 cm.) Bisque shoulder head with oval slender face and elongated throat, very white complexion, light brown sculpted hair loosely waved away from face into framed rolls of curls at the back of the head, and decorated with garlands of gold beads, painted bright blue eyes, red and black upper eyeliner, single stroke brows, accented nostrils and eye corners, closed mouth with center accent line, blushed cheeks, muslin stitch-jointed body, leather arms, antique silk gown with lace trim, undergarments, leather boots. Condition: generally excellent. Comments: Germany, circa 1870. Value Points: rarity factors include brown hair, fancy coiffure, gold beaded trim. $800/1200

79. German Porcelain Doll with Fancy Black Hair in Snood

19" (48 cm.) Porcelain shoulder head with oval face, elongated throat, black sculpted hair in softly rolled curls loosely gathered into a roll low on the nape of neck and captured inside a modeled snood, painted facial features, bright blue eyes, red and black upper eyeliner, single stroke brows, accented nostrils, closed mouth with center accent line, blushed cheeks, kid lady body with stitch-jointing, kid arms with separately stitched fingers, nicely costumed in black velvet and lace. Condition: generally excellent, fingers worn on right hand. Comments: Germany, circa 1870. Value Points: fine quality porcelain with lustrous patina, rare coiffure. $600/900

80. German Black Haired Porcelain Lady with Smiling Expression

17" (43 cm.) Porcelain shoulder head with rounded face, black sculpted hair arranged in a multitude of arranged horizontal curls with fine stippling onto the forehead, painted facial features, blue eyes, red and black eyeliner, single stroke brows, closed mouth with upturned lip corners as though smiling, accent line between the lips, muslin stitch-jointed body, porcelain lower limbs, painted green boots, nicely costumed. Condition: generally excellent, finger tips rough. Comments: Germany, circa 1875. Value Points: beautiful face, rare model to find with black hair. $700/900

81. Four German Porcelain Miniature Bathing Dolls

Each is all-porcelain child posed standing with feet apart, arms held in front of body with tiny clenched fists; including all black naked baby with tightly curled short hair, black baby with modeled white smock decorated with blue ribbons; pink-tinted white baby with black finger curls, bare feet, antique dress; and black child with modeled shorts and sun hat. Condition: generally excellent, few minor paint rubs. Comments: Germany, circa 1880. Value Points: rare variations in miniature size of the popular so-called "Frozen Charlotte" dolls. $600/900

82. Rare German Porcelain Doll with Wooden Articulated Body

7" (18 cm.) Pink tinted porcelain shoulder head with black sculpted very short curly hair, painted facial features, sculpted ears, blue eyes, carved wooden body with tiny wais, dowel-jointing at shoulders and hips, porcelain lower arms and legs with dowel-jointed attachment, painted orange slippers. Condition: generally excellent. Comments: Germany, circa 1850. Value Points: very rare miniature doll in perfectly preserved condition, with exquisite detail of painted hair and facial features. $1100/1500

83. German All-Porcelain Bathing Doll in Knit Wear

9" (23 cm.) One piece all porcelain figure of standing baby, legs modeled apart, arms held in front in small semi-closed fists, pink tinted complexion, black sculpted hair, painted blue eyes, red eyeliner, single stroke brows, closed mouth, wearing antique knitwear suit. Condition: generally excellent. Comments: Germany, circa 1885. Value Points: appealing petite size with pink tinted complexion. $400/500

84. Largest Size German Porcelain Bathing Doll by Conta & Bohme

18" (46 cm.) One piece porcelain figure of standing child with legs modeled apart, arms held in front of body with semi-cupped fists, the thumb and forefinger forming a circle, pink tinted facial complexion, black sculpted hair with deeply comb-marked sculpting, stippling details around the forehead, painted blue eyes in deeply incised eye sockets, red and black upper eyeliner, single stroke brows, accented nostrils and eye corners, closed mouth with outlined lips, blushed cheeks and ears. Condition: generally excellent. Marks: 11/0 (on one foot, impressed mark on other). Comments: Conta & Bohme, circa 1890, the uniquely sculpted thumb and forefinger are indicative of that firm, as well as the faint foot impression. Value Points: largest size known of the so-called "Frozen Charlottes" whit exceptional quality of sculpting. $1100/1600

85. Rare German Pink Tinted Bathing Doll with Unusual Expression

11" (28 cm.) One piece porcelain standing child with all-pink-tinted complexion, unusual square-shaped face, black painted hair with stippling details, painted brown eyes, black upper eye-liner, lightly feathered brows, legs modeled apart, arms held in front of body with small fists. Condition: generally excellent. Comments: Germany, circa 1880. Value Points: delightful character with unusual expression; other rarity factors include brown eyes and all-pink-tinting. $600/900

86. German Porcelain Bathing Doll with Original Costume

16" (41 cm.) One piece all-porcelain child in standing pose, legs apart, arms held in front of body with small folded fists, brown painted hair with stippling details around the forehead, pink tinted complexion, grey painted upper glancing eyes, thick black eyeliner, accented nostrils and eye corners, closed mouth with center accent line. Condition: generally excellent. Comments: Germany, circa 1880. Value Points: rarer brown hair and grey eyes, pink tinting, and wearing wonderful original knit bathing costume with cap and shoes. $800/1200

87. German Porcelain Bathing Doll with Pink Tinting Overall

14" (36 cm.) One piece porcelain figure of standing child, legs modeled apart and arms held in front of body with semi-closed fists, all-over pink tinting, light brown sculpted hair with comb-marked detail, matching color lightly feathered brows, painted blue eyes with shaded details, red and black upper eyeliner, closed mouth with prim lips, unusual body shape with shapely ankles, realistic feet. Condition: generally excellent. Comments: Germany, circa 1875. Value Points: rarity factors include unusual body mold, pink tinting, rare hair color, rare expression. $800/1100

and not 117n. Value Points: the very rare open-mouth variation of their classic 117 "Mein Liebling" model, with unusual original body variation, finest quality matte bisque, the exceptional size is largest K*R known to exist. $7000/10,000

89. German Bisque Character, 1295, by Franz Schmidt

17" (43 cm.) Bisque socket head, brown glass sleep eyes, dark eyeliner, painted lashes, brush-stroked brows, accented eye corners, pierced nostrils, open mouth, shaded and outlined lips, two porcelain upper teeth, tongue, brunette flocked hair, composition bent limb baby body. Condition: generally excellent, wig sparse. Marks: 1295 F.S. & C. 15. Comments: Franz Schmidt, circa 1915. Value Points: pretty gentle-faced character with lovely bisque, antique baby gown and bonnet. $500/700

90. English Blue and White Staffordshire Tea Set "Girl with Cat and Dog"

5" (13 cm.) teapot. Of creamy softpaste with blue transfer design depicting a little girl sitting on a stoop, a kitten in her arms, a nearby kitten lapping milk, and a dog seated at attention, with geometric borders. The service comprises lidded teapot, creamer, lidded sugar, 3 bowls, 4 plates, each marked Staffordshire England. Generally excellent, few minor flakes, creamer is darkened. Circa 1875. $400/500

88. Very Rare German Bisque Child, 117, by Kammer and Reinhardt in Exceptional Size

44" (112 cm.) Bisque socket head, brown glass sleep eyes, dark eyeliner, painted curly lashes, slightly modeled brows with brush-stroked and feathered detail, accented eye corners, shaded nostrils, open mouth, shaded and accented lips, four porcelain teeth, blonde mohair wig, composition and wooden ball-jointed body with elongated above-the-knee lower legs, well costumed in antique white-wear frock, undergarments, stockings, shoes. Condition: generally excellent, some body repaint. Marks: K&R Simon & Halbig 117 112 (back of head) 22.X 27/00 (crown rim). Comments: Kammer and Reinhardt, circa 1912, note that the model is 117

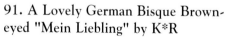

91. A Lovely German Bisque Brown-eyed "Mein Liebling" by K*R

21" (53 cm.) Bisque socket head, brown glass sleep eyes, painted curly lashes, short feathered brows, accented nostrils and eye corners, closed mouth with downcast pouty expression, accent line between the lips, brunette mohair wig, composition and wooden ball-jointed body, nicely costumed in antique cotton school dress, undergarments, stockings, shoes, straw bonnet. Condition: generally excellent. Marks: K*R Simon & Halbig 117/A 53. Comments: Kammer and Reinhardt, "Mein Liebling" from their transition art character series, circa 1912. Value Points: very dear sweet-faced child with wistful expression, lovely bisque and painting, original body finish. $4000/5000

92. Very Rare 44" German Bisque Child, 117, by Kammer and Reinhardt in Boy's Antique Woolen Suit

44" (112 cm.) Bisque socket head, large brown glass sleep eyes, thick dark eyeliner, painted dark lashes, thick brush-stroked brows with feathered details, accented eye corners and nostrils, open mouth, four porcelain teeth, brunette mohair wig, composition and wooden ball-jointed body with elongated lower legs that extend to above the knees. Condition: generally excellent. Marks: K*R Simon & Halbig 117 Germany 112 (back of head) 22.X 27/00 (crown rim). Comments: Kammer and Reinhardt, circa 1912, note that the model is the rare 117 open mouth (not the later 117n). Value Points: extraordinary size is largest known to exist for this very rare model, original body and body finish, fine quality bisque and painting, wearing wonderful antique woolen suit and top hat. $7000/10,000

93. Very Beautiful German Bisque Child with Closed Mouth by Kestner, Size 16

28" (71 cm.) Bisque socket head, large blue glass sleep eyes, thick dark eyeliner, painted lashes, brush-stroked and feathered brows, accented nostrils and eye corners, closed mouth with accented lips, brunette human hair wig with original plaster pate, composition and wooden ball-jointed body. Condition: generally excellent. Marks: made in Germany 16. Comments: Kestner, circa 1890. Value Points: beautiful large closed mouth child with pretty bisque, original body, rose flannel antique dress with lace collar, undergarments, rose silk bonnet, rose socks and shoes. $2200/2800

94. The Miniature Playthings of Mrs. Henry Endicott of Boston

5" (13 cm.) mirror. A collection of tiny playthings that once belonged to Mrs. Henry Endicott of Boston includes a fancy soft metal mirror with bracket frame, paper candy container in the

shape of a piano with silver candle holders, soft metal silver cruet set with glass bottles, two all-bisque dolls in soft metal gilded fancy cradles, fancily painted tin birdcage, ormolu six-arm chandelier, handmade cloth doll with painted face, small china Frozen Charlotte, and a little all-bisque doll with handmade costume. Condition: generally excellent. Comments: circa 1890, from the original family home of Mrs. Henry Endicott. Value Points: a delightful collection of miniature well-treasured playthings carefully preserved. $800/1000

95. German All-Bisque Doll Known as "French Wrestler"

8" (20 cm.) Bisque swivel head on kid-edged bisque torso, large blue glass inset eyes, painted short lashes and brows, accented nostrils, closed mouth, blonde mohair wig, shapely torso, peg-jointed bisque arms and legs, modeled bent left arm, very muscular and shapely legs with painted white ribbed stockings and yellow laced boots with black heels. Condition: generally excellent, tiniest neck socket chip (hidden), left elbow reglued. Marks: 2 (head). Comments: Kestner, circa 1885. Value Points: rare model with superb sculpting, wonderful face, swivel head, fancy boots, wearing her original multi-layered costume. $1200/1500

96. Very Large German Bisque Child with Closed Mouth by Kestner, Size 18

34" (86 cm.) Bisque socket head, large blue glass sleep eyes, thick dark eyeliner, painted lashes, rose blushed eye shadow, brush-stroked and feathered brows, accented nostrils, closed mouth with accent line between the shaded lips, brunette human hair wig in long ringlet curls over plaster pate, composition and wooden ball-jointed body. Condition: generally excellent, original body and body finish. Marks: made in Germany 18. Comments: Kestner, circa 1890. Value Points: unusually large model of the closed mouth series, with lovely luminous

bisque, enhancing decorative glaze on brows and lips, lovely antique white wear embroidered dress, undergarments, socks, shoes, cap. $3000/4000

97. Petite German Bisque Child with Closed Mouth by Kestner from Barrymore Estate

13" (33 cm.) Bisque socket head, brown glass sleep eyes, painted dark curly lashes, brush-stroked and feathered brows, accented nostrils and eye corners, closed mouth with accent line between the pouty lips, blonde mohair wig over plaster pate, composition and wooden ball-jointed body, antique white-wear dress, undergarments, lace cap, stockings, shoes. Condition: generally excellent, body repainted. Marks: 6/0. Comments: Kestner, circa 1885, from the original Barrymore estate of Philadelphia to the Carole Jean Zvonar collection. Value Points: pretty appealing petite child with expressive features, closed mouth, lovely costume. $1700/2300

99. An Early French Bisque Bébé Gigoteur with Steiner Signature on Torso

20" (51 cm.) Solid domed bisque head with flat-cut neck socket, rounded facial modeling with pale complexion, cobalt blue glass inset eyes, thick dark eyeliner, painted lashes, lightly feathered brows, mauve blushed eye shadow, open mouth with double row of teeth, brunette human hair wig, carton torso, kid-over-metal rod upper legs, composition lower legs and arms. When wound the bébé waves arms and legs in babylike fashion, turns head and cries "mama", wearing antique muslin chemise, stockings, blue leather shoes. Condition: generally excellent, arms are not original. Marks: Livre 17-11-66 J. Steiner (delivered November 17, 1866). Comments: Steiner's Bébé Gigoteur, one of the first models of this bébé that remained a popular doll for more than 25 years during the late 19th century. Value Points: especially beautiful face, Steiner signature. $2200/2800

100. Two Small German All-Bisque Dolls

5.5" (14 cm.) largest. Each is all-bisque with pale complexion overall, sculpted blonde hair and painted facial features, including smiling plump girl with black painted hair band, peg-jointed arms, and painted purple lustre boots; along with one piece standing girl in so-called Frozen Charlotte pose with blonde/brown painted curls. Condition: generally excellent. Comments: Germany, circa 1870. Value Points: rare to find models, rarity points on large includes jointed arms, coiffure, and lustre boots. $400/600

98. Beautiful French Bisque Bébé Schmitt with Original Signed Body

15" (38 cm.) Pressed bisque socket head with pear-shaped faced, very plump cheeks, blue glass enamel inset eyes with spiral threading, thick dark eyeliner, painted lashes, mauve blushed eye shadow, brush-stroked brows, accented eye corners and nostrils, closed mouth with defined space between the outlined lips, pierced ears, lambswool wig over cork pate, French composition and wooden eight-loose-ball-jointed body with straight wrists, flat-cut derriere, wearing antique pale green patterned silk dress with Alencon lace, undergarments, straw bonnet, aqua kidskin shoes marked "E.Jumeau". Condition: generally excellent. Marks: Sch (in shield) 1 (head) (shield mark on bottom of derriere). Comments: Schmitt et Fils, circa 1884. Value Points: lovely cabinet size bébé with well-sculpted features, beautiful eyes and bisque, original body and body finish. $8000/12,000

101. Earliest Period French Bisque Bébé Steiner with Original Body

16" (41 cm.) Bisque socket head with rounded facial shape, small pale blue glass enamel inset eyes, dark outline around the eyes, delicately painted lashes and feathered brows, mauve blushed eye shadow, accented nostrils and eye corners, closed mouth with outlined lips, pierced ears, original lambswool cap over Steiner pate with fleecy lambswool hair, Steiner composition full-jointed body with eight loose-ball-joints, straight wrists, cupped open fingers, antique muslin dress with lace edging and tiers, undergarments, socks, shoes,bonnet. Condition: generally excellent. Comments: Jules Steiner, a very early model bébé, circa 1875. Value Points: rare early model having beautiful bisque, expression, original body and costume, the doll was given to Carole Jean (then) Stoessel by her beloved grandmother Mom-Mom. $4000/6000

102. Ten Antique Doll Bonnets

To fit bébés about 12"-22". Of various styles and materials including wire-framed silk bonnets, woven straw, faux-fur mohair, and velvet, each bonnet is generously trimmed with silks, ribbons, laces and flowers to suit its appropriate style and era, and all have interior lining. Excellent condition. Circa 1890/1910. $600/900

103. Superb Petite French Bisque Bébé by Schmitt et Fils Known as "Cup and Saucer" Style

12" (30 cm.) Pale bisque head with flat-cut neck socket that joins to body by torso dowel, rounded facial shape, large pale blue enamel glass inset eyes with spiral threading, dark eyeliner, painted lashes, feathered brows, accented nostrils of tiny nose, accented eye corners, closed mouth with shaded and accented lips, rose eye shadow, pierced ears, blonde mohair wig over original Schmitt pate, original composition and wooden eight-loose-ball-jointed body with straight wrists, cupped fingers, flat-cut derriere. Condition: generally excellent. Marks: 3/0 Bte SGDG (head) (faint derriere impression) 000 (pate). Comments: Schmitt et Fils, circa 1878, their earliest model bisque bébé. Value Points: very rare Schmitt bébé in most appealing petite size, with original Schmitt wig, pate, body, body finish, silk dress and undergarments that are most likely original, rose silk antique bonnet, stockings, leather shoes with gold lettering "Bébé Jumeau Med d'Or Paris 4" and London doll boutique label of H.W. Morrell in Burlington Arcade. $9000/13,000

104. Beautiful Early French Bisque Bébé Steiner, Series A, in Rare Size

23" (58 cm.) Bisque socket head with rounded facial shape, very plump cheeks, large blue glass paperweight inset eyes, thick dark eyeliner, painted short lashes, brush-stroked fringed brows, rose blushed eye shadow, accented eye corners, shaded nostrils, closed mouth with pale accented lips, pierced ears, brunette mohair wig, cork pate, French composition fully-jointed body with straight wrists, lovely rose silk costume, undergarments, knit stockings, leather shoes with rosettes signed C.M. Condition: generally excellent. Marks: Sie A 4 (impressed) J. Steiner Bte SGDG J. Bourgoin (red ink script)

J. St. (and cadeceus symbol, on torso). Comments: Jules Steiner, circa 1882. Value Points: rarer model with wonderful childlike face, fine luminous bisque and large deep eyes, original body and body finish. $6000/7500

105. Ten Antique Doll Store Chemises

In various sizes and styles, of muslin or cotton, the original factory chemises were made for various French and German dolls, each trimmed in varying degrees of luxury with ribbons and/or lace. Very good/excellent condition. Late 19th century. $300/600

106. French Bisque Poupée as Normandy Nanny with Bisque Child

15" (38 cm.) Bisque swivel head on kid-edged bisque shoulder plate, blue glass enamel inset eyes, painted lashes, feathered brows, accented nostrils and eye corners, closed mouth with accented lips, pierced ears, blonde human hair over cork pate, shapely kid body with gusset-jointed elbows, stitched and separated fingers. Condition: generally excellent. Marks: F.G. (scroll) 2. Comments: Gaultier Freres, circa 1880. Value Points: with lovely bisque and very sturdy and firm original body, the

poupée is wearing her original costume of a Normandy nanny including original elaborate coiffe, black velvet edged cap, matching gown, apron, undergarments, black leather shoes, original Jumeau earrings, and is carrying little bisque doll with lavish silk and lace gown. $2500/3500

107. Exceptionally Large French Bisque Bébé Steiner, Figure C, with Lever Eyes

40" (102 cm.) Bisque socket head with plumply modeled cheeks, blue glass sleep eyes that operate from brass lever at back of head, dark eyeliner, painted lashes, brush-stroked fringed brows, rose blushed eye shadow, accented eye corners, shaded nostrils, closed mouth with outlined lips, pierced ears, brunette mohair wig over cork pate, French composition fully-jointed body. Condition: generally excellent. Marks: Figure C. No 8 J. Steiner Bte SGDG Paris (head) Le Petit Parisien Bébé Steiner (body) (eyes also signed Steiner). Comments:

Jules Steiner, circa 1888. Value Points: extremely rare largest size of the model, with original signed body and eyes, original body finish, lovely antique costume. $8000/11,000

108. Petite French Bisque Bébé Steiner in Lovely Costume

15" (38 cm.) Bisque socket head, blue glass paperweight inset eyes, dark painted eyeliner, painted lashes, fringed brows, accented eye corners and nostrils, closed mouth with outlined lips, pierced ears, brunette mohair wig, Steiner composition fully-jointed body with straight wrists, wearing lovely costume of rose organdy dress, and black velvet coat, hat and muff with rose silk satin bows, undergarments, stockings, shoes. Condition: generally excellent. Marks: J. Steiner Bte SGDG Paris Fre A 7 (head) (original Steiner paper label on torso). Comments: Jules Steiner, circa 1890. Value Points: very sweet-faced bébé with lovely bisque, original signed body. $3000/4000

109. Two Early Beaded Bonnets and Purses

To fit infant, the bonnets are finely woven and bead decorated. One is embroidered with small green beads, with note indicating that the bonnet was originally worn by Johan Carl Davidson (1771-1831), and the other is decorated with garlands of colorful beaded flowers. Along with small silk lined beaded purse with woven image of dog barking at the moon, and a woven reticule known as "miser's purse" with silver beadwork and silver belt loop. Excellent condition. Late 18th/mid-19th century. $300/500

110. Large Collection of Doll Corsets, Stays and Hoops

To fit various size dolls. Comprising four hoops for lady doll fashion including an unusual model with hoop support only at the bottom of the skirt, along with five corsets for lady dolls ranging from early poupées to ample-bosomed woman of the 1890's, and 14 additional corsets or stays for bébés and poupées in a variety of shapes and fabrics, some for Bébé Jumeau. Excellent condition. 1865/1900. $700/1100

111. Extremely Rare French Bisque Portrait Poupée with Ebony Complexion by Leon Casimir Bru

17" (43 cm.) Bisque swivel head on kid-edged bisque shoulderplate portraying a distinctively featured woman with ebony black complexion, large black enamel inset eyes, wide nose with upturned tip, painted black lashes and brush-stroked brows, open mouth, row of inset teeth, pierced ears, darkened kid poupée body with gusset-jointing, stitched and separated fingers, richly costumed in native fashion with wonderful textures and patterns. Condition: generally excellent, head, shoulderplate and body original. Comments: Leon Casimir Bru, the model was featured in *The Bru Book* by François Theimer (pp 170-175) indicated as an aristocratic Wolof woman of Senegal, Africa and an "utterly exceptional" doll, circa 1875, Value Points: the extraordinary sculpting of this magnificent doll is unique, the rich complexion tone enhanced by a lustrous patina, having superb original woven coiffe that perfectly frames the face. Few examples of this doll are known to exist. $10,000/15,000

112. Rare and Original French Bisque "Chinese Tea Server" by Leopold Lambert

20" (51 cm.) Standing upon a velvet covered wooden platform is a Chinese lady with rich amber tinted complexion, oval facial shape with modeled high cheekbones, narrow brown glass inset eyes, thick black eyeliner, lightly feathered brows and lashes, aquiline nose with flared accented nostrils, closed mouth with full accented lips, pierced ears, black mohair wig over cork pate, carton torso and legs, wire upper arms, amber tinted bisque forearms. When wound, the lady elegantly turns her head side to side in an upward sweep, tentatively nods, lifts right arm to pour tea (twice), offers the cup of tea, pauses and repeats, while music plays. Condition: generally excellent, mechanism and music function well. Marks: L.B. (key) (scraps of original tune label on base). Comments: Leopold Lambert, circa 1888, the piece appears in his original catalog as #39 described as "Chinois Verseuse" and having "tete caracterisee". Lambert commissioned the unique "character face" from Jumeau and was likely quite proud of this. It appeared on no other automaton or doll ever located to date. Value Points: extremely rare model with outstanding quality of sculpting and finest bisque and complexion with lustrous patina, original perfect hands, superb royal purple silk kimono with embroidered flowers. The doll is said to be from the early doll collection of 19th century actress Sarah Bernhardt. $12,000/18,000

113. An Outstanding and Extremely Rare French Bisque Asian Child by Leon Casimir Bru

20" (51 cm.) Amber tinted bisque swivel head on matching kid-edged bisque shoulder plate with modeled bosom and shoulder blades, amber brown glass paperweight inset eyes, thick dark eyeliner, black painted lashes with slight curl and extended length lash at outer edge of each eye, shaded brown brush-stroked and fringed bows in unique upward curved wing-tipped shape, rose blushed eye shadow, accented eye corners, shaded nostrils, closed mouth with defined space between the shaded lips, pierced ears, black mohair wig over cork pate, original kid bébé body, kid-over-wooden upper arms, amber tinted bisque forearms, wooden lower legs. Condition: generally excellent, finish on feet retouched. Marks: Bru Jne 7 (head and shoulder plate) (original paper label on chest). Comments: Leon Casimir Bru, Chevrot epoch, circa 1885. Value Points: the extreme rarity of this model is rivalled by its superb quality and remarkable state of preservation, having flawless bisque with luminous patina, artistic painting of features, perfect hands, superb antique silk embroidered costume, jewelry, hair flowers. Few models are known to exist, and it is likely that the doll was created by special commission only. $30,000/45,000

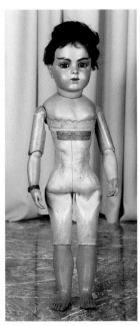

113 front nude.

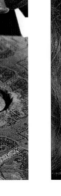

114 details.

114. Very Rare French Musical Mechanical Scene by Phalibois with Numerous Movements

21" (53 cm.) h. overall. 23"l. 15" standing doll. Posed upon an ebony wooden platform that hides the mechanical and musical movements are three bisque-headed dolls, each with blue glass eyes, painted facial features, closed mouth, pierced ears, mohair wig, carton torso, wooden or paper mache hands and feet with applied shoes. The center standing doll depicts a conjuror who is standing behind a magical table with three cones or shells; the two flanking dolls are seated in musician pose, one with violin, one with cello. When wound, and lever released, two tunes of very fine musical quality play, and a series of complicated movements occur in alternating and synchronic paths; the conjuror sweeps her hand as though calling for attention, nods downward, lifts the shells (sometimes singly, sometimes in unison) to reveal a number of different "surprises" hidden beneath, each suggesting a rare gem, except for a die which appears periodically. Meanwhile the musicians play their instruments, nodding and turning their heads. Condition: generally excellent. Comments: Phalibois of Paris, circa 1875, a duplicate piece with slight costume variations is in the Guinness Collection at the Morris Museum and is shown in *Automata, The Golden Age* by Bailly. Value Points: very rare luxurious automaton as indicated by three figures, fine music, portrait quality bisque faces, and wonderful original detail of costumes and accessories including textured floor that matches the table top. $20,000/30,000

115. Early Carved Wooden Doll on Wooden Plinth

12" (30 cm.) One piece carved wooden head, torso and legs of woman with modeled female torso, oval shaped face in slightly inclined pose, brown enamel eyes set in heavily lidded eye sockets, painted lashes and feathered brows, aquiline nose, closed mouth with center accent line on lips, elongated throat, brunette human hair, dowel-jointed shoulders and elbows, very expressively carved fingers, posed on original tiered wooden plinth. Condition: generally excellent. Comments: Continental, late 18th century. Value Points: superbly preserved original finish on the beautifully sculpted lady with articulated arms. $1200/1700

116. French Mannequin with Bisque Head and Rare Articulated Wooden Hands

38" (97 cm.) Bisque head with unique neck construction designed to accommodate mannequin body, brown glass paperweight inset eyes, thick dark eyeliner, lushly painted lashes, brush-stroked brows, accented nostrils and eye corners, closed mouth, accented lips, brunette mohair wig, on original mannequin body with black muslin cover, carved wooden lower legs and feet with defined ankle boots, carved wooden lower arms and hands with elaborately detailed articulation of fingers. Condition: generally excellent. Marks: F.G. (scroll on head) 6 Stockman Paris Brevete SGDG

116 detail.

4 (body). Comments: the Parisian mannequin creator, Stockman, with original Gaultier head, circa 1890. Value Points: wonderful smaller size mannequin with carved wooden boots, superb detail of hand articulation, especially pleasing facial model. $6000/8000

117. Larger French Bisque-Head Mannequin with Gaultier Head

49" (124 cm.) Bisque head with neck shape designed to accommodate to mannequin torso, brown glass paperweight eyes, dark eyeliner, painted lashes, widely brush-stroked brows, accented eye corners, shaded nostrils, closed mouth with accented lips, brunette human hair, black muslin covered mannequin armless body, cast iron boots, black velvet cape and cap in page boy style. Condition: generally excellent. Marks: F.G. (scroll). Comments: probably Stockman, Paris, circa 1890. Value Points: fine quality bisque, rare cast iron boots. $4000/5000

119. Rare Petite German Bisque Doll, Model 134, by Kestner with Brown Complexion

9" (23 cm.) Bisque socket head with rounded facial modeling and rich brown complexion, brown glass sleep eyes, black painted lashes, black brush-stroked brows, accented nostrils, open mouth with coral shaded lips, four porcelain teeth, black mohair wig, brown composition and wooden ball-jointed body. Condition: generally excellent. Marks: 134 2/0. Comments: Kestner, circa 1900. Value Points: superb petite doll with very beautiful bisque and flawless complexion with luminous highlights, original fully-jointed body with original finish, wonderful antique costume, undergarments, straw bonnet, socks, shoes. $800/1200

118. Extremely Rare German Bisque Three-Faced Doll Representing Three Ethnicities

14" (36 cm.) A bisque socket head enclosed at the sides and the back with a cardboard hood has three different faces that are alternately revealed when the brass knob at the top is turned: an ebony black face with crying expression, brown glass eyes, closed mouth with modeled tongue, sculpted tears; a light brown face with slightly smiling expression, brown glass eyes, and closed mouth; and a white face with modeled shut eyes and closed mouth. The hood is attached to a composition shoulderplate, muslin covered carton torso with pull-string "mama" crier, muslin upper legs, composition lower arms and legs. Condition: generally excellent, slight paint rub on chin of brown face. Marks: C.B. (in circle on shoulderplate) 450 dep (on top of heads). Comments: Carl Bergner, with original bisque faces by Bahr and Proschild, circa 1892. Value Points: extremely rare variation of the multi-face doll with beautiful expressions and complexions, original body. $2500/3500

120.

120. German Bisque Doll with Brown Complexion, Model 277, by Bahr and Proschild

12" (30 cm.) Bisque socket head with sienna brown complexion, brown glass inset eyes, black painted lashes and brows, accented nostrils and eye corners, open mouth with coral shaded lips, row of porcelain teeth, pierced ears, black mohair wig, brown composition body with jointing at shoulders and hips, painted yellow shoes. Condition: generally excellent. Marks: 277 dep 3. Comments: Bahr and Proschild, circa 1895. Value Points: rarely found early child doll, especially with brown complexion, wonderfully sculpted features and beautiful bisque, original body, original costume. $600/900

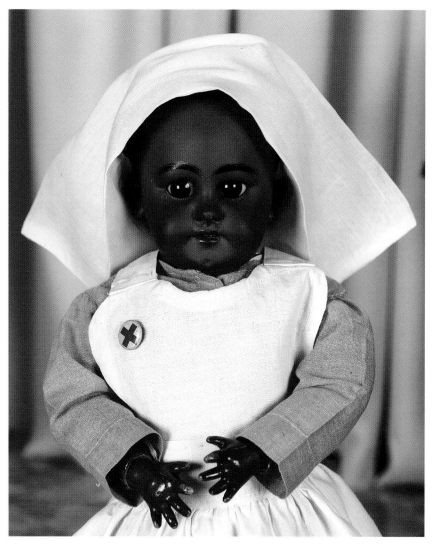

121.

121. Rare German Brown Bisque Character, 251, by Schutzmeister & Quendt with Flirty Eyes

16" (41 cm.) Bisque socket head with rich brown complexion, brown glass sleep and "flirty" eyes, black painted lashes, black feathered brows, rounded upturned nose with accented nostrils, open mouth, full coral-shaded lips, two porcelain upper teeth, black fleecy hair, brown composition bent limb baby body, antique dress, straw hat, knit booties, undergarment. Condition: generally excellent. Marks: 251 SQ Germany 8. Comments: Schutzmeister & Quendt, circa 1915. Value Points: very rare model, previously undocumented, with beautiful complexion and painting, original body and body finish. $2000/3000

122. German Bisque Character Baby, 251, by Schutzmeister and Quendt with Ebony Complexion

20" (51 cm.) Bisque socket head with ebony black complexion, unique sculpted ethnic features, small brown glass sleep eyes,

black painted lashes and brows, accented nostrils of small rounded nose, open mouth with full lips, two porcelain upper teeth, black fleecy hair, black composition baby body, antique red cotton pinafore dress, knit stockings. Condition: generally excellent, few small wig flakes (under wig). Marks: 251 SQ (intertwined). German 10 1/2. Comments: Schutzmeister & Quendt, circa 1915. Value Points: beautiful complexion enhances the highly characterized features; the doll is previously undocumented in doll literature. $1200/1800

123. Rare German Brown-Complexioned Bisque Doll, 1029, by Simon and Halbig

18" (46 cm.) Bisque socket head with rich brown complexion and elongated facial modeling with full cheeks, brown glass sleep eyes, black painted lashes and brush-stroked brows, accented nostrils and eye corners, open mouth, shaded and outlined lips, four porcelain teeth, pierced ears, black mohair fleecy wig, brown composition and wooden ball-jointed body. Condition: generally excellent. Marks: SH 1029 8 (incised) D.R.P. 56562 (red stamp). Comments: Simon and Halbig, circa 1890. Value Points: rare model, virtually unknown with brown complexion, having lovely painting, original body and body finish, antique nursing costume. $1800/2500

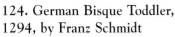

124. German Bisque Toddler, 1294, by Franz Schmidt

22" (56 cm.) Bisque socket head, blue glass sleep eyes, painted curly lashes, brush-stroked and feathered brows, accented nostrils, open mouth, outlined lips, two porcelain upper teeth, tongue, brunette mohair wig, composition and wooden ball-jointed toddler body with side-hip jointing. Condition: generally excellent. Marks: 1294 50. Comments: Franz Schmidt, circa 1915. Value Points: very choice bisque with lustrous patina, original wig, toddler body in great original condition, costume may be factory original and includes three little silver coins in matching purse. $700/900

125. German Bisque Character, 1070, by Konig and Warnecke

16" (41 cm.) Bisque socket head, blue glass sleep eyes, painted long curly lashes, short feathered brows, accented eye corners,

open mouth, slightly downcast pouty lips, two porcelain upper teeth, brunette mohair bobbed wig, composition bent limb baby body. Condition: generally excellent. Marks: K&W 1070 9. Comments; Konig and Warnecke, circa 1912. Value Points: appealing character model wears his original red knit baby dress, sweater, undergarments, socks, shoes and carries a little silver whistle. $600/800

126. Large German Bisque Toddler, 680, by Kley and Hahn

24" (61 cm.) Bisque socket head with rounded chubby face, blue glass sleep eyes, painted curly lashes, brush-stroked and feathered brows, accented nostrils and eye corners, open mouth, shaded and outlined lips, two porcelain upper teeth, tongue, antique brunette human hair wig in braids, composition and wooden ball-jointed body with side-hip jointing and very chubby torso. Condition: generally excellent. Marks: 266 680 8 K&H Made in Germany. Comments: Kley and Hahn, a model from their 600 series that is previously undocumented, circa 1915. Value Points: rare toddler with wonderful expression and bisque, fabulous body with fine original finish, cotton pinafore dress, undergarments, knit stockings, shoes appear original. $800/1200

127. Large German Bisque Child, 1078, by Simon and Halbig with Brunette Mohair Wig

36" (91 cm.) Bisque socket head, blue glass sleep eyes, painted lashes, brush-stroked brows, accented nostrils and eye corners, open mouth, four porcelain teeth, pierced ears, brunette mohair wig, composition and wooden ball-jointed body, wearing antique red cotton pinafore dress, blouse, undergarments, shoes, stockings. Condition: generally excellent. Marks: 1078 Germany Simon & Halbig S&H 16. Comments: Simon and Halbig, circa 1900. Value Points: grand-sized doll with lovely bisque and painting, impressed chin dimple and sculpted detail of brows, original body and original body finish, original wig. $1200/1500

128. Grand-Sized German Bisque Child, 1079, by Simon and Halbig with Unusual Expression

36" (91 cm.) Bisque socket head, large blue glass sleep eyes, painted curly lashes, widely brush-stroked and feathered brows, accented eye corners and nostrils, open mouth, shaded and accented lips, four porcelain teeth, pierced ears, (new) blonde human hair wig, composition and wooden ball-jointed body, wearing antique rose cotton pinafore over cotton dress, undergarments, shoes, stockings. Condition: generally excellent. Marks: 1079 17 S&H dep Germany. Comments: Simon and Halbig, circa 1900. Value Points: unusually expressive features with gentle appearance, fine quality bisque, deeply impressed chin dimple, sculpted brows, original body and body finish. $1200/1800

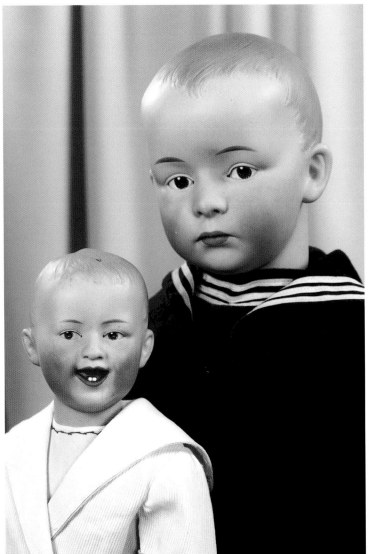

130. Large German Bisque Pouty, 7602, with Painted Eyes by Gebruder Heubach

30" (76 cm.) Bisque socket head with pink tinting, solid dome, blonde sculpted hair with blonde forelock curl, modeled "stuck-out" ears, dark blue intaglio eyes with large black pupils and white eyedots, black and red upper eyeliner, short feathered brows, accented nostrils and eye corners, closed mouth with downcast pouty expression on the shaded lips, composition and wooden ball-jointed body, costumed in navy blue sailor suit. Condition: generally excellent. Marks: 11 58 Heubach (sunburst) 7602 Germany. Comments: Gebruder Heubach, circa 1910. Value Points: fine large size of the wistful character boy has excellent bisque and modeling. $1100/1500

131. German Bisque Laughing Character, 7604, by Gebruder Heubach

19" (48 cm.) Solid domed bisque socket head with pink tinted complexion, blonde sculpted short boyish hair with comb-marked detail, intaglio blue eyes, white eyedots, short feathered brows, accented nostrils and eye corners, closed mouth modeled as though open with shaded and accented lips, two beaded lower teeth, composition and wooden ball-jointed body, nicely costumed in antique mariner style boy's suit. Condition: generally excellent. Marks: 7604 Heubach (sunburst mark) 6 Germany. Comments: Gebruder

129. Large German Bisque Pouty Character, 7246, with Glass Eyes by Gebruder Heubach

32" (81 cm.) Pink tinted bisque socket head, brown glass sleep eyes, painted curly lashes, incised eyeliner, brush-stroked fringed brows, accented nostrils and eye corners, closed mouth with center accent line, brunette mohair wig, composition and wooden ball-jointed body, costumed in navy blue sailor suit, leggings, black patent leather shoes. Condition: generally excellent. Marks: 13 7246 Heubach (square) Germany. Comments: Gebruder Heubach, circa 1915. Value Points: rare large size of the wonderful wistful character with very choice bisque, original body finish. $3000/4000

Heubach, circa 1912. Value Points: expressive appealing features enhanced by fine quality of bisque, original body finish with pull-string crier. $700/900

132. German Bisque Character with Mechanical Walking Body by Gebruder Heubach

9" (23 cm.) Solid domed bisque socket head with painted blonde baby hair, painted blue intaglio eyes, lashes and brows, closed mouth modeled as though open with beaded teeth, carton ball-shaped body with small metal spoked wheels, composition arms, original muslin gown. Condition: generally excellent. Marks: Heubach (square) Germany 7404 (?). Comments: Gebruder Heubach, probably for Zinner and Sohne, circa 1910, when wound, the doll glides along, turning, glides again. Value Points: amusing simple mechanical toy works well, great character face. $700/900

133. Grand German Bisque Character Pouty with Mechanical Movements by Gebruder Heubach

25" (64 cm.) Pink tinted bisque socket head, blue glass eyes, dark eyeliner, painted curly lashes, thickly brush-stroked fringed brows, accented nostrils, closed mouth with center accent line between

the downcast pouty lips, blonde mohair bobbed wig, composition bent limb body. Condition: generally excellent. Marks: 13 7246 Heubach (square mark) Germany. Comments: Gebruder Heubach, circa 1912, when keywound, the mechanism hidden inside torso causes the eyes to blink open and closed, and the head to turn from side to side. Value Points: rare model whose rarity is increased by internal mechanism, very choice bisque and sculpting, wearing original wonderful costume of young dandy comprising shirt with wide lace collar, velvet pants, striped knit stockings, leather boots, woolen beret. $3000/4000

134. Very Rare German Bisque Mechanical Baby by Gebruder Heubach

16" (41 cm.) Pink tinted bisque socket head, blue glass eyes, painted lashes and brows, accented nostrils and eye corners, open mouth, accented lips, two porcelain teeth, tongue, blonde mohair wig, composition bent limb baby body, antique costume. Condition: generally excellent, mechanism functions well. Marks: 10557 7 Heubach (in square). Comments: Gebruder Heubach, circa 1920, the body is fitted with keywind mechanism that, when wound, causes the doll to open and close its eyes, stick-out its tongue, and lift and lower its right arm. Value Points: expressive laughing face is enhanced by amusing mechanism movements that function well. $1200/1800

135. Beautiful Large German Bisque Character Baby by Kestner

25" (64 cm.) Solid domed bisque socket head, painted blonde baby hair with sculpting detail at the crown, large brown glass sleep eyes, painted dark curly lashes, brush-stroked and feathered brows, shaded nostrils, open mouth, shaded and accented lips, two porcelain teeth, tongue, composition bent limb baby body. Condition: generally excellent. Marks: K made in Germany 12 (head) Made in Germany (body). Comments: Kestner, circa 1915. Value Points: superb condition of the grand-sized baby with outstanding sculpting and bisque, original body and body finish, outstanding antique baby gown and undergarments. $800/1100

136, 137, 138.

136. Largest German Porcelain Bathing Doll with Conta & Bohme Signature

18" (46 cm.) One piece all-porcelain very chubby child in standing pose, with legs modeled apart, arms held in fronf of body with small folded fists, the thumb and and forefinger forming a small circle, blonde sculpted hair with highly defined combmarks, painted blue eyes in deeply set eye sockets, red and brown upper eyeliner, feathered brows, accented nostril circles and eye corners, closed mouth with bow-shaped lips, blushed cheeks, sculpted ears. Condition: generally excellent. Marks: (Conta & Bohme trademark on foot). Comments: Germany, circa 1890. Value Points: rare largest size of the so-called Frozen Charlotte doll has outstanding quality of sculpting, maker's mark. $900/1300

137. German Pink Tinted Porcelain Bathing Doll

15" (38 cm.) One piece all-porcelain pink-tinted doll in standing pose, legs modeled apart, arms held in front of body with folded fists, blonde sculpted hair with comb-marked detail, painted pale blue eyes, red and black upper eyeliner, lightly feathered brows, accented nostrils and eye corners, closed mouth with accent line between the lips, sculpted ears, blushed cheeks. Condition: generally excellent. Comments: Germany, circa 1880. Value Points: rarity factors include sculpting of hair, pink tinting, well-detailed body features, unusual size. $600/900

138. German Pink-tinted Bathing Doll with Black Hair

13" (33 cm.) One piece porcelain doll posed standing with legs slightly apart and arms held in front with small folded fists, all pink-tinted complexion, black painted hair with excellent sculpting detail, stippling lines around the hair edges, painted blue upper glancing eyes, red and black upper eyeliner, single stroke brows, circle accents at nostrils, closed mouth with center accent line. Condition: generally excellent. Comments: Germany, circa 1880. Value Points: rare size enhanced by pink tinted porcelain, wonderful body detail particularly knees, toes, fingers, nails, and knuckles. $500/800

139. Very Beautiful German Bisque Character "Lori" by Swaine and Co with Peach Complexion

20" (51 cm.) Solid domed bisque socket head with delicate peach-toned complexion, blue glass sleep eyes, delicately painted lashes and brows, accented nostrils and eye corners, closed mouth with defined space between the shaded lips, blonde painted baby hair with delicate stippling, composition bent limb baby body. Condition:

generally excellent. Marks: Lori 2 (incised) Geschutz S&Co Germany (green stamp). Comments: Swaine and Co, circa 1915. Value Points: rare model with exquisite painting and detail of modeling, original body and body finish, fine antique costume. $2000/3000

140. Larger German Bisque Character "Lori" by Swaine and Co with Pale Complexion

22" (56 cm.) Solid domed bisque socket head with pale bisque and blushed cheeks, blue glass sleep eyes, dark painted curly lashes, incised eyeliner, brush-stroked and feathered brows, accented eye corners and nostrils, closed mouth modeled as though open, shaded lips, blonde painted baby hair, composition bent limb baby body, antique baby gown and bonnet. Condition: generally excellent. Marks: Lori 1 (incised) Geschutz S&Co Germany (green stamp). Comments: Swaine and Co, circa 1915. Value Points: excellent detail of modeling enhanced by lovely bisque and painting, original body and body finish. $2000/3000

142. French Bisque Mechanical Walking Doll with Roller Mechanism in Feet

23" (58 cm.) Bisque socket head, brown glass flirty eyes, painted lashes, brush-stroked and feathered brows, accented nostrils and eye corners, open mouth, shaded and accented lips, four porcelain teeth, pierced ears, blonde mohair wig, French body with large carton torso containing chain-drive clockwork mechanism that activates the tiny wheels hidden in the base of her feet, composition and wooden fully-jointed body. Condition: generally

141. Very Fine French Wax Mannequin Child in Original Costume

41" (104 cm.) Wax socket head with blue glass paperweight inset eyes, inserted upper and lower eye lashes and brows, accented nostrils, closed mouth with accented lips, blonde human hair in boyish style inserted into scalp, on original mannequin body with black muslin cover, cast iron feet, jointed arms. The mannequin is wearing a child's antique Cossack trousers and shirt under lush silky mohair winter coat and matching cap. Condition: generally excellent. Comments: French, circa 1890. Value Points: outstanding mannequin with exquisite detail of face, cast iron boots, wonderful costume. $2000/3000

144.

excellent, faint vertical line on forehead, hands repainted. Marks: 1039 Germany Halbig S&H 10 1/2. Comments: Fleischmann and Blodel, with original Simon and Halbig head, when keywound, the doll "walks" along, flirts. Value Points: beautiful large example of the "roller" walking doll wearing antique red mohair coat and bonnet. $1500/1800

143. French Bisque Mechanical Walking Doll by Roullet et Decamps

16" (41 cm.) Bisque socket head, blue glass flirty eyes set on glass rod, mohair lashes, painted lower lashes, brush stroked and multi-feathered brows, rose blushed eye shadow, accented nostrils and eye corners, open mouth, shaded and accented lips, four porcelain teeth, pierced ears, blonde mohair wig over cork pate, French carton torso containing clockwork mechanism, one piece "walking" legs, composition fully-jointed arms. Condition: generally excellent. Marks: 79 10 Handwerck (incised) Wimpern (red stamp on head). Comments: Roullet et Decamps, circa 1900, when keywound, the doll alternately lifts her legs and appears to move along. Value Points: beautiful cabinet size doll has lovely bisque, flirty eyes, mohair lashes and wig, walking action, and wears red mohair coat and beret to match her larger sister. $1500/2500

144. German Bisque Child, 1039, by Simon & Halbig for the French Market

22" (56 cm.) Bisque socket head, blue glass sleep eyes, painted curly lashes, dark eyeliner, brush-stroked and feathered brows, accented nostrils, open mouth, shaded and outlined lips, four porcelain teeth, pierced ears, (new) brunette human hair wig in ringlet curls, French composition and wooden fully-jointed body. Condition: generally excellent. Marks: 12 SH 1039 dep (head, with Wimpern stamp) Bébé Jumeau Diplome d'honneur (body stamp). Comments: Simon and Halbig for Jumeau/SFBJ, circa 1900. Value Points: the pretty child wears her original dress, undergarments, woven straw bonnet with lining, shoes and stockings. $500/800

145. French Bisque Automaton "Winter Girl" with Snow Bird" by Roullet & Decamps

23" (58 cm.) Standing upon a teal green velvet covered platform is a bisque-headed child with blue glass eyes, mohair lashes, painted lower lashes, brush-stroked brows, accented eye corners and nostrils, open mouth, four porcelain teeth, pierced ears, wheat blonde human hair wig over cork pate, carton torso and legs with separating panel at chest level, wire upper arms, right bisque forearm. The doll is costumed in a white fur coat with matching muff and winter cap, and has leather leggings and shoes. Condition: generally excellent, mechanism and music function well, one finger reglued. Marks: SH 1039 10 1/2 dep (incised). Comments: Roullet & Decamps, circa 1900, when the presentation begins the little girl stands shyly with both hands hidden inside the muff. When wound and lever released, she quickly blinks her eyes several times, then looks to each side and nods; she lifts the muff, and her right hand escapes holding in it a little red feathered bird. She shows the bird from side to side, blinks again, and pauses. Periodically she "breathes", as though shivering, with heaving chest. Music plays throughout. Value Points: a rare and wonderfully intricate automaton with simple yet appealing theme is well preserved and functions well. $6000/9000

mohair wig, composition and wooden ball-jointed body with unusual shaping including 2nd and 3rd fingers molded together. Condition: generally excellent, faint hairline on forehead. Marks: 79 5n Germany. Comments: Handwerck, circa 1910. Value Points: the pretty child wears her original muslin chemise with lace trim, has original wig, body, body finish. $400/500

148. German Bisque Child by Heinrich Handwerck with Rare Hair Eyebrows for this Model

32" (81 cm.) Bisque socket head, blue glass sleep eyes, painted lower lashes, mohair lashes, cut eyebrows with original hair inserts to simulate look of real brows, accented eye corners and nostrils, open mouth, accented lips, four porcelain teeth, pierced ears, auburn mohair wig, composition and wooden ball-jointed body, wearing pretty lace dress, undergarments, stockings, shoes. Condition: generally excellent. Marks: Germany Heinrich Handwerck Simon & Halbig 7 . Comments: Handwerck, circa 1910. Value Points: rare inserted eyebrows for this maker, lovely bisque, original body and body finish, the actual doll is shown in Simon and Halbig Dolls, The Artful Aspect by Foulke, page 214. $700/1000

149. Beautiful German Bisque Child by Heinrich Handwerck from Original Owner

27" (69 cm.) Bisque socket head, blue glass sleep eyes, dark eyeliner, dark painted curly lashes, short brush-stroked and feathered

146. Grand-sized German Bisque Child by Heinrich Handwerck

42" (107 cm.) Bisque socket head, blue glass sleep eyes, dark eyeliner, painted long curly lashes, brush-stroked brows with sculpted detail and comb-marks, accented nostrils and eye corners, open mouth, accented lips, four porcelain teeth, pierced ears, antique hand-tied brunette human hair wig, composition and wooden ball-jointed body, antique dress with lace Bertha collar, undergarments, socks, shoes. Condition: generally excellent, body repainted. Marks: Germany Heinrich Handwerck Halbig 9. Comments: Handwerck, circa 1900. Value Points: rare large size allowing beautiful expression of features, lovely bisque. $1400/1800

147. Petite German Bisque Child, 79, by Handwerck in Original Chemise

14" (36 cm.) Bisque socket head, brown glass sleep eyes, painted lashes and brows, accented nostrils and eye corners, open mouth, accented lips, four porcelain teeth, pierced ears, brunette

brows, accented nostrils and eye corners, open mouth, shaded and outlined lips, four porcelain teeth, dimpled chin, pierced ears, brunette mohair wig, composition and wooden ball-jointed body. Condition: generally excellent. Marks: Germany Heinrich Handwerck Simon& Halbig 5 (head) Heinrich Handwerck (body). Condition: generally excellent. Value Points: all original one-owner doll prior to its acquisition by Carole Jean Zvonar, the doll has beautiful matte bisque, original soft mohair wig, original body and body finish, beautiful lace dress, undergarments, stockings, leather shoes. $600/800

150. German Bisque Child by Heinrich Handwerck with Original Chemise and Label

38" (97 cm.) Bisque socket head, brown glass sleep eyes, dark eyeliner, dark painted curly lashes, slightly modeled brush-stroked brows, accented eye corners, shaded nostrils, open mouth, shaded and accented lips, four porcelain teeth, pierced ears, brunette human hair antique wig, composition and wooden ball-jointed body. Condition: generally excellent, hands retouched. Marks: 79 171/2 Germany Handwerck 8 (head) Heinrich Handwerck (body). Comments: Handwerck, circa 1900. Value Points: the beautiful large child wears her original muslin chemise with original paper label "Genuine Heinrich Handwerck Doll", has original signed head and body, lovely bisque and wig. $1100/1500

152. Three German All-Bisque Dolls with Sculpted Costumes

6.5" (17 cm.) largest. Each is all bisque with painted facial features and costume, including girl with country style costume, rare bare feet and brunette mohair wig; Native American with flocked finish on costume to suggest suede, side glancing eyes and sculpted head-dress; and impish girl with sculpted fur hat, collar and muff, painted shoes and socks, otherwise nude, standing as though shivering. Condition: generally excellent. Comments: Germany, circa 1910. Value Points: interesting variety of modeled-costume all-bisque dolls. $400/500

153. An Outstanding Pair of German Bisque Characters "Max" and "Moritz" by Kammer and Reinhardt

15" (38 cm.) Each has bisque socket head with uniquely sculpted face depicting a mischievous lad, small brown glass flirty eyes, very thick brown or black "comma" shaped brows with sculpting detail, laughter crinkles around the eyes, upturned rounded nose with accented nostrils, beaming smile on closed mouth, accented lips, impressed dimples, flax wigs (Moritz with stiffened red wig having topknot curl), uniquely sculpted body with jointing at shoulders, elbows, hips and knees, pointing fingers, sculpted stockings and shoes with upturned toes. Condition: generally excellent. Marks: K*R Simon & Halbig 123 (or 124). Comments: Kammer and Reinhardt, circa 1913, the uniquely modeled urchins were sculpted for the doll firm to represent the popular characters Max and Moritz, originally created by the German author Wilhelm Busch in the mid-19th century, and later immortalized for the American market in the comic strip "The Katzenjammer Kids". The comic strip was created in 1897 by German immigrant Rudolph Dirks for the Hearst newspaper syndicate. In 1912 Dirks and Hearst became involved in a legal wrangle, resulting in Dirks leaving Hearst and creating a rival comic strip "Hans und Fritz" (basically the same characters), while Hearst continued "The Katzenjammer Kids" although drawn by another artist. The actual doll models were registered by Kammer and Reinhardt in the German courts in 1913, and it seems logical that their production may have been inspired by this legal battle, as a means of Hearst continuing to promote the Max and Moritz names, although this fact is not currently documented. Value Points: among the rarest of the German character series, the pair have distinctive sculpting, superb bisque, original distinctive bodies, Moritz with factory original costume. The pair was originally owned by a German butcher in Philadelphia who had bought them when new, passed to one other owner before being acquired for the Zvonar Collection. $40,000/65,000

151. German Bisque Laughing Character, 116/A by Kammer and Reinhardt

18" (46 cm.) Bisque socket head, small blue glass sleep eyes, painted curly lashes, short feathered brows, accented nostrils and eye corners, closed mouth modeled as though open with defined tongue, shaded lips, two upper beaded teeth, brunette mohair wig, composition and wooden ball-jointed toddler body with side-hip jointing. Condition: generally excellent, hands retouched. Marks: K*R Simon & Halbig 116/A 42. Comments: Kammer and Reinhardt, circa 1912, from the transitional era of their art character series. Value Points: very choice modeling and bisque on the cheerful toddler, original wig, great antique costume. $1800/2800

154. Exceptionally Large German Bisque Child, 949, by Simon and Halbig, Size 18

42" (107 cm.) Bisque socket head with elongated modeling and very full lower cheeks, brown glass sleep eyes, thick dark eyeliner, painted curly lashes, thick brush-stroked and feathered brows, accented eye corners, shaded nostrils, open mouth, shaded and accented lips, four porcelain teeth, pierced ears, antique hand-tied brunette human hair wig, composition and wooden ball-jointed body, beautiful (frail) antique dress with richly embroidered colorful flowers, undergarments, shoes, stockings. Condition: generally excellent, some body retouch. Marks: SH 18 949. Comments: Simon and Halbig, believed to be the largest size of this model, circa 1890. Value Points: very rare grand-sized doll with lovely bisque and painting, original body, fine antique costume. $3000/4000

155. An All-Original German Bisque Doll, 1009, By Simon and Halbig

12" (30 cm.) Bisque socket head, brown glass sleep eyes, painted lashes and feathered brows, accented nostrils and eye corners, open mouth, four porcelain teeth, pierced ears, blonde mohair wig in long braids, composition and wooden ball-jointed body. Condition: generally excellent. Marks: 1009 Halbig German S&H 5. Comments: Simon and Halbig, circa 1890. Value Points: the petite doll wears her original Swiss regional costume with beautiful lace coiffe and velvet vest, apron, skirt, blouse, original shoes and stockings, original wig with hip-length braids. $600/900

156. German Bisque Fashion Lady, 949, by Simon and Halbig in Original Wedding Gown

19" (48 cm.) Bisque swivel head on kid-lined bisque shoulder plate, slender facial modeling with full cheeks, brown glass inset eyes, dark painted lashes, short brush-stroked brows, accented

eye corners, shaded nostrils, closed mouth with downcast pouty lips, dimpled chin, pierced ears, brunette mohair wig in upswept fashion, kid gusset-jointed fashion body with slightly elongated torso, bisque forearms in unusual attachment so only thumbs touch the sides of the gown. Condition: generally excellent. Marks: S 9 H 949. Comments: Simon and Halbig, circa 1885. Value Points: acquired by Carole Jean Zvonar from its original New Hampshire family owners, the closed mouth, swivel head lady wears her original (frail) ivory silk satin wedding dress. $2000/2500

157. Delightful French Bisque Automaton "Young Girl with Seashell and Flute" by Roullet & Decamps

20" (51 cm.) Standing upon a velvet covered platform that contains a music box and clockwork mechanism is a bisque head doll having brown glass eyes, painted lower lashes, feathered brows, accented nostrils and eye corners, open mouth, accented lips, four porcelain teeth, pierced ears, brunette mohair wig, carton torso and legs, wire upper arms, composition forearms. She is wearing a navy blue mariner costume with peach silk trim with matching cap, and holds a coral sea shell in her right hand and a flute in her left hand. Condition: generally excellent. Marks: 1300-6 Dep S&H (doll) (fragments of original paper tune on base). Comments: Roullet & Decamps, circa 1900. When wound and lever released, the little girl brings the flute to her lips as though playing to call the mermaids, nods and turns her head, plays again, and then brings the sea shell to her ear to listen to the ocean; music plays. Value Points: rare automaton with delightful activity and beautiful state of preservation. $5500/7500

158. Rare French Bisque Musical Automaton "Lady of the Court" by Leopold Lambert

20" (51 cm.) Standing upon a velvet covered platform (disguised by her long gown) is a bisque-headed doll with blue glass paperweight inset eyes, lushly painted dark lashes, widely arched brush-stroked brows, rose blushed eye shadow, accented nostrils, closed mouth, white mohair wig in late 18th century style coiffure, carton torso and legs, wire upper arms, bisque forearms. The doll is costumed as a Marquise of the Royal court in blue satin with crepe de chene borders and holds a powder puff in one hand and mirror in the other. Condition: generally excellent, mechanism and music function well, glass of mirror is lacking. Marks: Depose Tete Jumeau 4 (doll) L.B. (key) Carmen Danse (tune label). Comments: Leopold Lambert, circa 1890, the uniquely designed automaton achieved its ladylike stature by cascading the gown over the platform base, Value Points: beautiful and rare automaton with lovely music, exquisite appearance with original wig and costume; from the Samuel Pryor collection before its acquisition by Carole Jean Zvonar. $7000/9500

159. Wonderful French Bisque Bébé E.J. by Jumeau in Appealing Size 2

10" (25 cm.) Pressed bisque socket head, deep blue glass paperweight eyes, dark eyeliner and lushly painted lashes, brush-stroked brows, accented nostrils and eye corners, closed mouth with outlined shaded lips, pierced ears, brunette mohair wig over cork pate, French composition and wooden fully-jointed body with straight wrists, with antique undergarments, silk dress, old socks and shoes, lace cap. Condition: generally excellent. Marks: Depose E. 2 J (head) Jumeau Medaille d'Or Paris (body).

Comments: Emile Jumeau, circa 1884. Value Points: most endearing petite bébé with beautiful expression and bisque, original body and body finish. $5000/7500

160. French Bisque Bébé Jumeau, Size 9, with Lovely Silk Costume

21" (53 cm.) Bisque socket head, blue glass paperweight inset eyes, lushly painted lashes, thick brush-stroked and feathered brows, accented eye corners and nostrils, closed mouth, outlined shaded lips, pierced ears, antique brunette hand-tied human hair wig over cork pate, French composition and wooden fully-jointed body with pull-string "mama" crier. Condition: generally excellent. Marks: Depose Tete Jumeau Bte SGDG 9 (and artist checkmarks). Jumeau Medaille d'Or Paris (body). Comments: Emile Jumeau, circa 1890. Value Points: pretty bébé with original body and body finish, lovely French silk dress, velvet bonnet, undergarments, leather shoes. $3500/4000

161. French Bisque Poupée with Beautiful Grey Eyes

17" (43 cm.) Bisque swivel head on kid-lined bisque shoulder plate, grey glass enamel inset eyes, dark eyeliner, delicately painted lashes and feathered brows, accented nostrils and eye corners, closed mouth with outlined lips, pierced ears, blonde mohair wig over cork pate, French kid gusset-jointed poupée body with shapely torso, stitched and separated fingers, nicely costumed in ice blue silk gown, undergarments, leather boots, woven bonnet. Condition: generally excellent. Marks: 3 (head and shoulder plate). Comments: Gaultier, circa 1875. Value Points: very pretty classic poupée with original wig and body. $2000/2500

162. Beautiful French Bisque Bébé Jumeau with Brilliant Eyes

34" (86 cm.) Bisque socket head, very deep blue glass paperweight inset eyes, very thick black eyeliner, lushly painted lashes, thick brush-stroked and feathered brows, accented eye corners, shaded nostrils, open mouth, shaded and outlined lips, row of porcelain teeth, pierced ears, antique brunette hand-tied human hair wig of waist length, cork pate, French composition and wooden fully jointed body. Condition: generally excellent. Marks (artist checkmarks). Comments: Emile Jumeau, circa 1890. Value Points: an exceptional example of the open-mouth Jumeau bébé with superb creamy bisque and transfixing eyes, original Jumeau body, beautiful antique silk dress, undergarments, straw bonnet, Jumeau socks, old shoes with original box. $3000/4000

163. Rare and Enchanting French Bisque Mechanical "Flower-Seller with Basket of Fruits and Flowers" by Vichy

12" (30 cm.) A bisque-headed young lad with swivel head on bisque shoulder plate, blue glass enamel inset eyes, painted lashes and feathered brows, closed mouth with accented lips, brunette mohair wig over cork pate, carton torso, wire upper arms and legs, bisque forearms, paper mache lower legs, is standing behind a cart with three metal spoked wheels which supports a French woven market hotte laden generously with dried and silk fruits and flowers that the lad is offering for sale; the doll is attached to the cart by a metal rod into his body. When wound, the young man walk briskly along, pushing his cart, head turning side to side. Condition: generally excellent. Comments: Gustav Vichy, circa 1870. Value Points: delightful mechanical doll functions well, has original elaborate silk costume and decorations. $4000/6000

164. Beautiful French Bisque Bébé by Emile Jumeau with Transitional Model Face

23" (58 cm.) Pressed bisque socket head, brown glass paperweight eyes of great depth, thick dark eyeliner, painted curly lashes, widely-arched brush-stroked brows with enhancing decorative glaze, accented eye corners, shaded nostrils, closed mouth with shaded and outlined lips, separately

modeled pierced ears, auburn mohair wig over cork pate, French composition and wooden eight-loose-ball-jointed body with straight wrists. Condition: generally excellent, very light body retouch. Marks: 11 (head) Jumeau Medaille d'Or Paris (body). Comments: Emile Jumeau, circa 1880, the transitional model head appeared as both bébé and poupée models, and is considered rare. Value Points: beautiful and very expressive face with gorgeous bisque and painting, rich deep eyes, original body, lovely antique costume. $5500/7500

165. Rare French Bisque Automaton "Gentleman Smoker" by Leopold Lambert

23" (58 cm.) Bisque socket head, brown glass paperweight inset eyes, dark eyeliner, dark painted lashes, brush-stroked brows, accented nostrils and eye corners, very slightly parted lips although appearing as though closed mouth, pierced ears, blonde mohair wig over cork pate, carton torso and legs, wire upper arms with tubing for smoke passage, bisque forearms. Condition: generally excellent, smoking mechanism functions well. Marks: (Jumeau artist check marks on head) 2035/yo (paper label on base). Comments: Leopold Lambert, the smoking automaton was a favorite of that firm, offered in a variety of styles and sizes, with or without music, circa 1890. When wound, the Marquis appears to smoke, inhale and exhale from his especially sculpted mouth, through a complicated hidden mechanism; he alternately lifts lorgnette to his eyes as though to gaze at an interesting scene. Value Points: rare automaton with especially handsome appearance, very choice modeling of face, original magenta silk satin costume with gilt metallic embroidered vest, ormolu miniature lorgnette. $8000/11,000

166. Beautiful Large French Bisque Bébé Jumeau with Rich Brown Eyes

32" (81 cm.) Bisque socket head with plump cheek modeling, rich brown glass paperweight inset eyes, thick dark eyeliner, lushly painted dark lashes, widely arched brush-stroked and feathered brows, accented eye corners, shaded nostrils, closed mouth with defined space between the shaded and outlined lips, separately applied pierced ears, antique hand-tied brunette human hair wig, French composition and wooden fully-jointed body. Condition: generally excellent. Marks: Depose Tete Jumeau 14 (and artist checkmarks, on head) Bébé Jumeau Diplome d'Honneur (body). Comments: Emile Jumeau, circa 1886, one of the first tete models, having outstanding deep modeling of features, separately modeled ears unusual on this model. Value Points: very beautiful bébé whose sculpting includes dimples on philtrum and chin, fine lustrous complexion, deep eyes, original body and body finish, wonderful antique costume including leather shoes signed "Bébé Jumeau Depose 14". $4500/6500

of the rarest models from the character baby series, circa 1915, the actual doll is featured in *Simon & Halbig, The Artful Aspect* by Jan Foulke on page 174. Value Points: rare model with wonderful sculpting and finest quality bisque, the rare model is rarer yet in this grand size. $1800/2500

168. Very large German Bisque Character by Kammer and Reinhardt

25" (64 cm.) Bisque socket head, blue glass sleep eyes, painted curly lashes, brushstroked and multi-feathered brows, accented nostrils, open mouth, shaded and accented lips, two porcelain upper teeth, tongue, brunette mohair wig, composition bent limb baby body, wearing antique baby gown, undergarments, lace bonnet. Condition: generally excellent. Marks: K*R Simon & Halbig 22 Germany 62. Comments: Kammer and Reinhardt, circa 1915. Value Points: wonderful definition of sculpting and finest quality of bisque, original body and body finish. $700/1000

169. German All-Bisque Googly with Modeled Costume

4" (10 cm.) One piece all bisque figure of shy little boy with arms clasped to his side, brown sculpted hair, painted facial features, side-glancing googly brown eyes, shy impish smile, sculpted white smock. Condition: generally excellent. Comments: Germany, circa 1915. Value Points: wonderful expression, detail of decoration including blushed cheeks and knees. $300/400

170. Grand-Size German Bisque Character, 121, by Kammer and Reinhardt

24" (61 cm.) Bisque socket head, blue glass sleep eyes, thick dark eyeliner, painted curly lashes, short feathered brows, accented nostrils, open mouth, outlined lips, two porcelain upper teeth, tongue, brunette mohair wig, composition bent limb baby body. Condition: generally excellent. Marks: K*R Simon & Halbig 121 62. Comments: Kammer and Reinhardt, circa 1915. Value Points: lovely bisque and painting, well modeled features, original body finish, very fine antique gown with elaborate embroidery. $800/1000

167. Rare Large German Bisque Character, 118, by Kammer and Reinhardt

24" (61 cm.) Bisque socket head, small blue glass sleep eyes, painted curly lashes, brush-stroked and multi-feathered brows, accented nostrils, open mouth, shaded and accented lips, two porcelain upper teeth, impressed dimples in cheeks, chin and philtrum, brunette human hair bobbed wig, composition bent limb baby body, wearing lovely antique baby gown with embroidery, undergarments, peach silk organza bonnet. Condition: generally excellent. Marks: K*R Simon & Halbig 118 62. Comments: Kammer and Reinhardt, one

171. German Bisque Character, 128, by Kammer and Reinhardt

21" (53 cm.) Bisque socket head, blue glass sleep eyes, dark painted curly lashes, short feathered brows, accented nostrils, open mouth, outlined lips, two porcelain upper teeth, tongue, composition bent limb baby body. Condition: generally excellent. Marks: K*R Simon & Halbig 128 56. Comments: Kammer and Reinhardt, circa 1915. Value Points: one of the rarer character baby models of that firm, having beautiful matte bisque, fine antique gown, bib, undergarments, original body and body finish. $800/1000

172. Rare Doll-Sized Half-Tester Brass Bed, Possibly Salesman Sample

26" (66 cm.) l. 26"h. Of fine brass with fancily turned spindles, the brass bed features an unusually high canopy or tester headboard, original metal springs, and is beautifully fitted with antique linens and lace. The quality construction suggests its possible original purpose as a salesman's sample. Excellent condition. Circa 1890. $800/1200

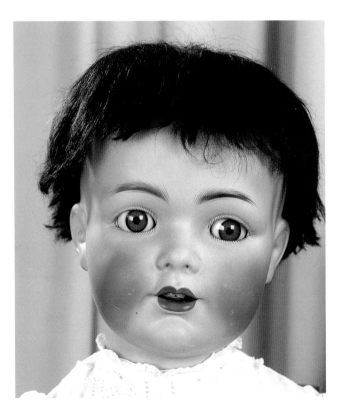

174. German Bisque Character with Brown Painted Eyes, 149, by Hertel and Schwab

15" (38 cm.) Bisque socket head, brown painted eyes with well-defined white eye dots, black and red upper eyeliner, short feathered brows, accented nostrils and eye corners, closed mouth with very full shaded lips, brunette mohair wig, composition and wooden ball-jointed body. Marks: 149 4. Comments: Hertel and Schwab, circa 1910. Value Points: very expressive features with beautiful eye painting, original body finish, great antique costume includes unusual felt novelty pincushion parasol. $2500/3500

175. German Bisque Character by Wiesenthal, Schindel & Kallenberg with Painted Eyes

11" (28 cm.) Solid domed bisque socket head, painted blonde baby hair with defined brush-strokes, painted facial features, small blue eyes, red and black eyeliner, short feathered brows, closed mouth with defined space between the outlined lips, composition bent limb baby body, antique costume. Condition: generally excellent. Marks: WSK 541 2. Comments: Bahr and Proschild for Wiesenthal, Schindel & Kallenberg, circa 1910. Value Points: rarely found model with unusually fine quality of sculpting for this smaller size, very fine bisque and painting, original body and body finish. $500/800

173. German Bisque Character, 526, with Painted Brown Eyes, by Kley and Hahn

20" (51 cm.) Bisque socket head, painted brown eyes with shaded color, black upper eyeliner, very short fringed lashes, feathered brows, accented nostrils, closed mouth with pouty expression, accent line between the lips, brunette human hair wig, composition and wooden ball-jointed body. Condition: generally excellent. Marks: K&H (in banner) 526 7 1/2. Comments: Kley and Hahn, circa 1912. Value Points: the rarer model has excellent bisque and painting, expressive features, original body and body finish, great antique costume. $3000/3500

176. German All-Bisque Snow Baby with Jointed Limbs

5" (13 cm.) Bisque head and torso with painted facial features, pin-jointed bisque arms and legs, the body and head (excepting face) completely covered in "snow" covered white hooded suit, mittens and feet are white bisque. Condition: generally excellent. Comments: Germany, circa 1915. Value Points: large size and jointed limbs. $300/400

177. German Bisque Character "Baby Stuart" by Gebruder Heubach

12" (30 cm.) Bisque socket head of young child with sculpted white Dutch bonnet decorated with delicate roses and trailing vines, incised holes at bonnet corners for insertion of ribbons, painted facial features, intaglio blue eyes, white eyedots, black upper eyeliner, short feathered brows, accented nostrils and eye corners, closed mouth with downcast lips, accent line between the lips, composition bent limb baby body, antique costume, holding tiny old golden teddy. Condition: generally excellent. Marks: Heubach (sunburst mark) Germany 7977.

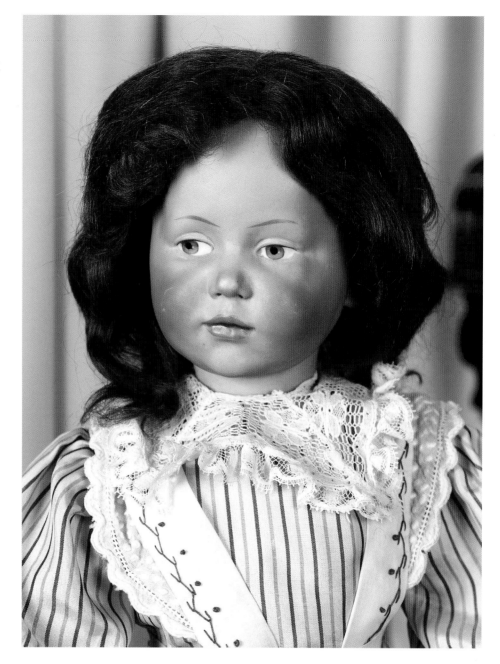

Comments: Gebruder Heubach, circa 1912, their model known as Baby Stuart. Value Points: very fine quality bisque and modeling on the sculpted cap pouty baby. $700/900

178. Especially Fine German Bisque Pouty "Marie", 101 by Kammer and Reinhardt with Side-Glancing Eyes

20" (50 cm.) Bisque socket head, painted blue eyes with right-glancing expression, thick black upper eyeliner, red upper eyeliner, short tapered brows, accented nostrils and eye corners, closed mouth with accented pale lips, brunette mohair wig, composition and wooden ball-jointed body, antique costume. Condition: generally excellent. Marks: K*R 101 50. Comments: Kammer and Reinhardt, circa 1910, the model "Marie" from their art character reform series. Value Points: especially fine detail of sculpting with very fine quality of complexion and modeling with deeply impressed facial features, choice bisque and painting, original body and body finish, unusual painting of eyes in side-glancing pose. $3500/4500

and Halbig, circa 1900. Value Points: beautiful doll with lovely complexion and expression, her presentation enhanced by fine antique costume, a rare model with brown complexion. $1100/1500

180. German Bisque Child Doll with Brown Complexion by Heinrich Handwerck

29" (74 cm.) Bisque socket head with light brown complexion, brown glass sleep eyes, black painted lashes, black thickly brush-stroked brows with feathered details and decorative glaze, accented nostrils and eye corners, open mouth, four porcelain teeth, pierced ears, black mohair wig, brown composition and wooden ball-jointed body. Condition: generally excellent. Marks: Germany Heinrich Handwerck Simon & Halbig 15. Comments: Handwerck, circa 1895. An interesting story is told about Handwerck's production of black dolls in Cieslik's *German Doll Studies*, page 203; their production was encouraged by Minna Handwerck (wife) who commissioned Simon and Halbig to manufacture "several adequate heads with pretty Negro faces of chocolate color and not deep black". Heinrich had little hopes for the dolls, but sales were heavy, production could hardly keep up with demand, and "this brought us a very good profit" said Minna. Value Points: rare large model with antique costume, acquired by Carole Jean Zvonar from "the oldest black resident of Edenton, North Carolina whose father was a minister". $1100/1500

181. A Smaller Model of German Bisque Brown-Complexioned Child by Handwerck

16" (41 cm.) Bisque socket head with brown complexion, brown glass sleep eyes, black painted lashes and feathered brows, accented nostrils and eye corners, open mouth, shaded lips, four porcelain teeth, pierced ears, black mohair wig, brown composition and wooden ball-jointed body. Condition: generally excellent. Marks: Heinrich Handwerck Simon & Halbig Germany. Comments: Handwerck, circa 1900. Value Points: an especially pretty petite model of Handwerck's brown-complexioned doll wearing antique maroon woolen dress, undergarments, argyle stockings, red shoes, red pressed flannel bonnet with feathers. $800/1000

179. German Bisque Child, 1079, by Simon & Halbig, with Brown Complexion

25" (64 cm.) Bisque socket head with rich dark brown complexion, large brown glass sleep eyes, painted black curly lashes, black sculpted and brush-stroked brows with decorative glaze, accented nostrils, open mouth, four porcelain teeth, pierced ears, black mohair wig, composition and wooden ball-jointed body, antique blue cotton dress, undergarments, saddle shoes, straw bonnet. Condition: generally excellent. Marks: S&H 1079 Dep Germany 11. Comments: Simon

182. Petite German Bisque Brown-Complexioned Doll, 1009, by Simon and Halbig

9" (23 cm.) Bisque socket head with light brown complexion, brown glass inset eyes, black painted lashes and brows, accented nostrils, open mouth with slightly parted lips, four tiny porcelain teeth, pierced ears, black fleecy hair, brown composition and wooden ball-jointed body with straight wrists, wearing antique cotton dress, printed apron, undergarments, shoes and socks. Condition: generally excellent. Marks: S 1 H 1009 dep St. Comments: Simon and Halbig, circa 1890. Value Points: rarer model, especially with brown complexion which is flawlessly presented in this example, appealing petite size. $600/900

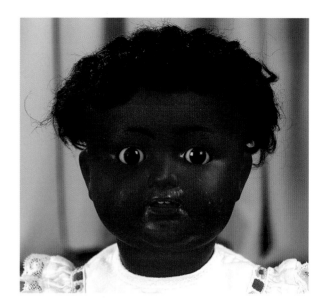

184. German Brown Complexion Baby by Adolt Hulss

18" (46 cm.) Bisque socket head with dark brown complexion portraying rounded face child, brown glass sleep eyes, black painted lashes and feathered brows, accented nostrils and eye corners, open mouth, two porcelain upper teeth, black fleecy mohair wig, brown composition bent limb baby body, antique costume. Condition: generally excellent. Marks: AHW (in circle) Simon & Halbig made in Germany. Comments: Adolf Hulss, circa 1920. Value Points: rarer model cheerful face, flawless complexion, original body and body finish. $700/1000

183. Rare German Bisque Character with Beautiful Brown Complexion

17" (43 cm.) Solid domed bisque socket head with rich brown complexion, painted black baby hair with decorative glaze, tiny brown glass sleep eyes, painted black lashes and short brows, accented nostrils, closed mouth with full lips, brown composition bent limb baby body, wearing antique checkered cotton dress with red hanky, undergarments. Condition: generally excellent. Marks: KB-M Germany 4. Comments: Germany, circa 1920. Value Points: rare model with beautifully expressive features, very fine bisque with flawless complexion, original body and body finish. $900/1400

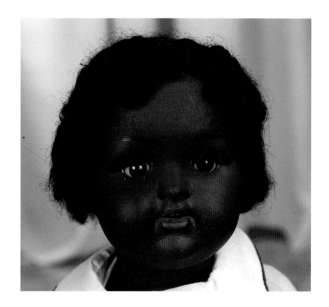

185. Rare German Bisque Character, 990, by Marseille with Rich Brown Complexion

18" (46 cm.) Bisque socket head with dark brown complexion, rounded plump toddler face, small brown glass sleep eyes, black painted lashes and brush-stroked brows, accented nostrils, open mouth, coral shaded lips, two porcelain upper teeth, black fleecy mohair wig, brown composition bent limb baby body, antique lilac romper suit. Condition: generally excellent. Marks: Armand Marseille Germany 990 A 7 M. Comments: Marseille, circa 1918. Value Points: very rare model to find with brown complexion, beautiful painting, original body and body finish. $1000/1500

186. Three German Porcelain Dolls with Black Complexion and Original Bodies

11" (28 cm.) largest. Each has porcelain shoulder head with ebony black complexion, sculpted hair in very tight short curls, painted features, brown muslin body. Condition: generally excellent. Comments: including 11" man with black upper glancing eyes, black porcelain lower limbs, wearing antique gentleman's suit; 10" boy with rare painted brown eyes, brown porcelain limbs; and 8" girl with painted limbs and defined boots, wearing country costume. Condition: generally excellent. Comments: Germany, circa 1890. Value Points: a rare trio with excellent detail of features, rare brown eyes on boy, the smallest bearing an award ribbon from Aunt Lenora Hoyte's Museum from where it was acquired by Carole Jean Zvonar. $900/1400

187. Rare German Bisque Doll with Brown Complexion and Sculpted Hair Attributed to Hertwig

13" (33 cm.) Bisque shoulder head with rich brown complexion, painted brown upper glancing eyes, outlined eyes, black single stroke brows, closed mouth, black sculpted hair with very tight short curls, brown muslin body,

bisque lower limbs with brown painted boots. Condition: generally excellent. Marks: 1. Comments: attributed to Hertwig, circa 1890. Value Points: rare model with outstanding detail of sculpting, very fine painting, antique calico dress, undergarments, cutwork apron. $900/1300

188. An All-Original American Cloth Alabama Baby by Ella Smith from Original Owner

18" (46 cm.) All cloth doll with hard pressed and oil painted shoulder head stitch-attached to torso, painted brown short curly hair in modified bobbed fashion, painted large brown eyes with very thick dark outline, curly painted all-around lashes, white eyedots, accented nostrils, closed mouth with pursed lips, blushed cheeks, stitch-jointed arms and legs, painted brown stockings and shoes. Condition: generally excellent. Marks: The Ella Smith Doll Co. (original stamp and patent label). Comments: Ella Smith, circa 1915. Value Points: beautiful original painting with lustrous patina, unusual brown shoes, wearing original red knit dress and cap, the doll was acquired by Carole Jean Zvonar from its original owner, May Sutphin of Winston-Salem, North Carolina. $1100/1500

189. Four Wonderful American Paper mache Hand Puppets from Philadelphia W.P.A. Artists

16" (41 cm.) Each is of light paper mache with hand-sculpting depicting storybook fantasy figure, with painted facial features, hollow cloth costume to disguise puppeteer's hand, cloth or paper mache hands. Condition: generally excellent. Marks: Museum Extension Project #20530 Philadelphia W.P.A. (on three puppets). Comments: the folk art puppet dolls were created by American artists during the Depression Years as part of the Federal Artist's project, Works Projects Administration (W.P.A.), circa 1935. Value Points: depicted are Grandmother, Wolf, and two children, the rare American folk art figures have wonderful detail of sculpting and painting. $1000/1500

190. American Wooden Doll by Mason-Taylor with Unusual Paper Mache Head

12" (30 cm.) Wooden-bodied doll with pin and dowel-jointing at shoulders, elbows, hips and knees, metal hands and feet, shapely torso, has solid domed paper mache head with glass inset eyes, lightly painted features. Condition: very good, finish on hands worn, feet repainted, paint wear at neck socket. Comments: Mason-Taylor doll, Vermont, the head appears original to the doll, although uncertain, circa 1880. Value Points: unique American doll whose past is a curious yet intriguing mystery. $800/1000

191. American Wooden Paint Decorated Doll's Chair with Maker's Signature

8" (20 cm.) One piece chip-carved wooden chair in barrel fashion with rounded back

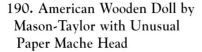

terminating in center peak, fanciful carved design at the front seat frame that extends all over the back, painted original black with stencilled scrolls and other designs in gold and red in the Pennsylvania German style. The chair is pencil signed inside "Johnson Hagen" and "600" in flowing script. Excellent condition. Mid-19th century. $400/500

192. German Paper Mache Doll Known as "Milliner's Model" in Original Gown

20" (51 cm.) Paper mache shoulder head with rounded facial shape, black sculpted hair arranged in uniform size finger curls, painted blue eyes, black upper eyeliner, painted brows, accented nostrils, closed mouth with center accent line, blushed cheeks, slender kid body with paper banding at elbows and knees, wooden lower arms and legs, painted flat green shoes. Condition: generally excellent, light craquelure to original finish. Comments: Germany, circa 1860. Value Points: early slender fashion lady with original finish, good early calico costume with transfer pattern, unusual buttons, undergarments. $800/1200

193. Large English Wooden Doll with Blue Enamel Eyes and Original Costume

26" (66 cm.) One piece carved wooden head and torso, egg-shaped head with oval face, elongated throat, flat-back torso with shaped bosom and tiny waist,

slender wooden legs with jointing at hips and knees, bare feet, tiny ankles, original red kid arms with stitched and separated fingers, inset blue enamel eyes with short fringed "dot" ashes, very thin "dot" brows, triangular-shaped pointy nose, closed mouth with center accent line, blushed cheeks, original (very sparse) wig and wig cap under brunette human hair wig. Condition: generally excellent, original finish, little nose rub. Comments: England, mid-18th century. Value Points: beautiful large model of classic English doll with original body and painting, the rose satin high-waisted gown with woven bonnet edged in rose satin, undergarments, appear original. $12,000/15,000

194. Petite English Wooden Doll with Provenance

12" (30 cm.) All wooden doll with egg-shaped oval head, high forehead, elongated throat, flat-back torso with shapely bosom and waist, simplistic wooden one-piece arms and legs, defined fingers, inset black enamel eyes with "dot" fringed lashes and brows, spot-blush on cheeks, tiny closed mouth, original wig cap with remnants of original hair. Condition: generally excellent, original paint well preserved with nose rub, wig sparse. Comments: England, late 18th century. Value Points: the doll wears an early olive green silk faille gown, petticoat, and has letter of provenance indicating that she was owned by the John Stevens family of Chester County, Pennsylvania in 1802. $5000/7000

195. Italian Terra Cotta Figure of Monk in Early Costume

8" (20 cm.) Terra cotta turned head, bald pate with sculpted tufts of hair with sideburns, painted facial features, large blue eyes, thick brows, closed mouth with beaded teeth, hemp-wrapped body with terra cotta hands and feet, painted sandals, wearing brown monk's robe. Condition: very good. Comments: early 19th century. Value Points: fine detail of sculpting on early characterized face. $400/500

196. French Bisque Poupée in Original Walnut Framed Presentation

12" (30 cm.) doll. 22"width of frame. A walnut-framed octogan shaped shadow-box with gilded lining contains a bisque swivel-head fashion lady with blue eyes, painted facial features, closed mouth, pierced ears, blonde mohair wig over cork pate, French kid gusset-jointed body with stitched and separated fingers. Condition: generally excellent. Marks: 0. Comments: Gaultier, circa 1875. Value Points: in a beautiful state of preservation with near mint firm body, the poupée wears her original costume and is presented with a garland of silk flowers where she has been presented for 130 years. $2000/3000

197. An Unusually Fine and Large Chinese Carved Figure of Lady with Jewelry and Flower

12" (30 cm.) Reclining on a teakwood plinth is a carved ivory lady with elaborate and intricate carving of hair, body posture, facial features, shoes and other ornamentation, having tiny beaded eyes, clasping a large sunflower, and having sculpted beaded necklace and bracelet inset with tiny colored beads, as well as a "loose" matching bracelet. Condition: generally excellent. Comments Chinese, late 19th century, the figures are known as "doctor's dolls" indicating their possible use by modest women to point out ailing parts of body; the elaborate ornamentation of this model suggests rather its creation as a decorative object. Value Points: very fine carving including unusual flower and jewelry designs. $2000/3000

198. Large German Porcelain Doll with Brown Eyes

30" (76 cm.) Porcelain shoulder head with short black curly hair having centerpart and casually arranged curls overall, painted brown eyes with dark outline, red and black upper eyeliner, single stroke brows, accented eye corners and nostrils, closed mouth with primly set lips, old muslin hand-made stitch-jointed body, Condition: generally excellent. Comments: Germany, circa 1880. Value Points: the large brown-eyed doll has early body, wears fancy silk gown with silk buttons, undergarments, shoes. $600/900

199. German Porcelain Doll with Brown Eyes

23" (58 cm.) Porcelain shoulder head with black sculpted hair arranged in short finger curls, painted brown eyes, black upper eyeliner, single stroke brows, accented eye corners and nostrils, closed mouth with accent line between the lips, (new) muslin body and porcelain limbs. Condition: generally excellent. Comments: Germany, circa 1885. Value Points: rarer brown eyes. $500/700

200. American Mechanical Walking Doll "Autoperipatetikous"

10" (25 cm.) Porcelain shoulder head with black sculpted hair with wide wing curls at sides of head drawn into loosely braided coil at nape of neck, painted bright blue eyes, red and black eyeliner, single stroke brows, closed mouth, blushed cheeks, carton torso and skirt-shaped base with protruding brass "feet", leather arms, porcelain hands, wearing antique white gown. Condition: generally excellent, functions well. Marks: Patented July 15, 1862.... Comments: Autoperipatetikous, one of the first patented American toys, 1862, the mechanism is hidden under the skirt, and when wound, causes the doll to glide forward on brass feet. Value Points: rare early American toy, with original porcelain head, beautifully detailed and rare coiffure, acquired by Carole Jean Zvonar from the Samuel Pryor Collection. $1200/1500

201. German Porcelain Doll Head with Fancy Coiffure

6" (15 cm.) Porcelain shoulder head with slender oval face, elongated throat, black sculpted hair in loose curls waved away from face into loosely coiled braid at back of head, blue eyes, red and black upper eyeliner, single stroke brows, accented nostrils of aquiline nose, closed mouth. Condition: generally excellent, original firing line at front shoulderplate. Comments: Germany, circa 1870. Value Points: lovely elegant lady whose pink tinted complexion enhances the hand-pressed detail. $400/500

202. Rare German Porcelain Lady with Dresden Flowers and Earrings

20" (51 cm.) Porcelain shoulder head with oval facial shape, elongated throat, sculpted bonnet that covers the complete back of head and forms a frame around the face, the bonnet decorated with blue, yellow and rose flowers and leaves in the Dresden manner, fully modeled ears with applied Dresden flower earrings, painted blue eyes, red and black upper eyeliner, single stroke brows, accented nostrils, closed mouth, (newer) muslin body with porcelain limbs, painted lustre boots, early muslin gown, undergarments. Condition: generally excellent, hairlines on replaced legs, small chip at bottom back corner of shoulder plate. Comments: Germany, circa 1885. Value Points: rarity factors includes Dresden bonnet and Dresden earrings. $900/1300

203. Two German Porcelain Figures with Dresden Decorations

6" (15 cm.) Each is a one piece porcelain figure of man and woman on self base, with sculpted and colorfully painted costume and Dresden style decorations. Condition: generally excellent, man has flake on hat rim, few Dresden flakes. Marks: (each has maker's stamp). Comments: mid-19th century. Value Points: exquisite detail of porcelain decoration. $400/500

204. German Porcelain Doll with Rare Brown Hair and Smiling Expression

19" (48 cm.) Porcelain shoulder head with rounded facial shape, light brown ("cafe-au-lait") hair in elaborately sculpted horizontal curls that taper to delicate curls

onto the forehead and cascade at back of head, painted blue eyes, black upper eyeliner, single stroke brows, accented nostrils, closed mouth with delicate hint of smile, blushed cheeks, old muslin body, bisque forearms and lower legs, fancily painted pink and green boots, antique costume. Condition: generally excellent, fingers on left hand broken. Comments: Germany, circa 1875. Value Points: wonderful detail of hair sculpting, rare brown hair, fancy boots. $500/800

205. Exquisite Miniature Porcelain Bust with Script Label

5" (13 cm.) Porcelain bust on plinth depicting a beautiful woman with long brown flowing ringlet curls and tightly woven braided coil at the back of head, painted brown eyes, eyeliner, single stroke brows, closed mouth, modeled bosom, modeled blue low-bodiced blouse with shaded decorations. Condition: generally excellent. Marks: (blue stamp) Mlle de Laveilles (?, red ink script). Comments: mid-19th century. Value Points: beautiful porcelain work on diminutive portrait figure. $400/600

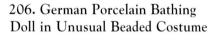

206. German Porcelain Bathing Doll in Unusual Beaded Costume

5" (13 cm.) One piece porcelain figure of standing child with legs apart, arms held in front of body, sculpted black hair in pageboy fashion, painted facial features, tiny blue eyes, red and black eyeliner, accented nostrils, eye brows, closed mouth with tiny pertly shaped mouth. Condition: generally excellent. Comments: Germany, circa 1880. Value Points: the so-called "Frozen Charlotte" wears his original beaded costume with fitted jacket, blue trousers, colorful collar and cuffs, brown shoes. $300/400

207. German Black Haired Porcelain Lady with High Forehead

24" (61 cm.) Porcelain shoulder head with black sculpted hair in casually arranged curls, painted blue eyes, red and black upper eyeliner, single stroke brows, accented nostrils, closed mouth, new muslin body with porcelain arms, antique porcelain lower legs with sculpted green boots decorated with black tassel and tips, blue velvet gown with lace trim. Condition: generally excellent. Comments: Germany, circa 1885. Value Points: fine quality of porcelain with nicely blushed cheeks. $400/500

209. German Porcelain Lady with Sculpted Black Curly Hair

28" (71 cm.) Porcelain shoulder head with rounded facial modeling, slightly elongated throat, short black sculpted curly hair in tousled fashion, partially sculpted ears, large blue painted eyes, red and black upper eyeliner, thick one stroke brows, accented eye corners, shaded nostrils, closed mouth with accent line between the full lips, muslin stitch-jointed body, kid arms with stitched and separated fingers, black taffeta gown with crocheted trim, undergarments. Condition: generally excellent. Comments: Germany, circa 1885. Value Points: large size china has fine lustrous china, beautifully shaped nose, unusually large eyes and lips. $600/900

208. German Black Haired Porcelain Doll with Sloping Shoulders

31" (79 cm.) Porcelain shoulder head with rounded facial shape, deeply sloping shoulder plate, black sculpted hair in short curls, painted facial features, bright blue eyes, red and black upper eyeliner, single stroke brows, circle accent nostrils, closed mouth with center accent line, muslin stitch-jointed body, porcelain limbs, painted boots, wearing black velvet beaded gown, undergarments. Condition: generally excellent. Comments: Germany, circa 1885. Value Points: fine lustrous patina of porcelain. $500/700

210. Rare German Porcelain Doll with Amber-Tinted Complexion

12" (30 cm.) Porcelain shoulder head with black sculpted hair in short curls (so-called "common" hairdo), amber tinted complexion, painted brown eyes, black upper eyeliner and brows, accented nostrils, closed mouth with center accent line, muslin stitch-jointed body, porcelain lower arms, painted boots, wearing original hand-stitched and embroidered Eastern folklore costume. Condition: generally excellent. Comments: Germany, circa 1890. Value Points: rare complexion and brown eyes, original costume. $500/700

211. German Black Haired Porcelain Doll with Elaborate Coiffure

19" (48 cm.) Porcelain shoulder head with rounded facial shape, black sculpted curly hair with tightly clustered curls surmounted by sculpted flowers at the crest, painted facial features, pale blue eyes, red and black upper eyeliner, single stroke brows, accented nostrils of tiny nose, closed mouth, muslin body, porcelain limbs, unusual colorful folklore style costume. Condition: generally excellent. Marks: 6. Comments: Germany, circa 1885. Value points: unusual coiffure with rich black color of hair. $500/800

212. Large German Black Haired Porcelain Doll with Feedsack Torso and Early Costume

31" (79 cm.) Thick paste porcelain shoulder head with slight pink tinting, black sculpted curls that frame the face and form vertical finger curls at the back of the head, painted large royal blue painted eyes, black and red upper eyeliner, single stroke brows, circle accents at nostrils, closed mouth with center accent line, old muslin stitch-jointed body with feedsack cloth printed torso, kid arms. Condition: generally excellent. Comments: Germany, circa 1880. Value Points: excellent detail of sculpting definition, well defined nose, unusual color eyes, wearing wonderful linen dress with soutache trim, undergarments, leather slippers. $700/1000

213. Large German Black Haired Porcelain Lady with Pink Tinted Complexion

34" (86 cm.) Porcelain shoulder head with delicately pink tinted complexion, short black sculpted curls, painted facial features, blue eyes, red and black upper eyeliner, single stroke brows, circle accents at nostrils, closed mouth with primly set lips, (new) muslin stitch-jointed body and porcelain limbs, cotton calico gown with lace collar, undergarments. Condition: generally excellent. Comments: Germany, circa 1885. Value Points: large size model, pink tinted complexion. $500/800

213.1. Early Muslin Gown with Handmade lace Trim

To fit lady doll about 26". Of very sheer delicate muslin, the rounded neck gown features pouf sleeves, set-in waist band that is hidden at the front with a full-length set in panel framed with bands of blue silk overlaid with handmade lace, gathers at the back for fit. Excellent condition. Mid-19th century. $400/500

hair hand-tied wig over cork pate, French kid poupée body with shapely torso, gusset-jointed limbs, stitched and separated fingers and toes, wearing indigo blue handwoven fitted gown, undergarments, beautiful early tablier with embroidery, ruffled cap, shoes. Condition: generally excellent. Marks: Brevete SGDG (body stamp). Comments: Blampoix, the brevete mark likely referred to his depose for glass eyes, circa 1865. Value Points: rare early glass eyed French poupée with beautiful luminous complexion enhanced by delicately tinted blush, original signed body. $6000/8000

215. French Bisque Poupée by Gaultier with Fine Antique Costume

15" (38 cm.) Bisque swivel head on kid-edged bisque torso, large blue glass enamel inset eyes, dark eyeliner, dark painted lashes, feathered brows, accented nostrils and eye corners, closed mouth with pale accented lips, pierced ears, blonde mohair wig over cork pate, French kid poupée body with gusset jointing, stitched and separated fingers. Condition: generally excellent. Marks: 4 F.G. (head and shoulders). Comments: Gaultier, circa 1875. Value Points: unusually large blue eyes enhances the expressive features, wearing beautiful antique blue/grey taffeta two piece gown, undergarments, slippers, bonnet, earrings. $2000/2500

214. Beautiful Early French Poupée with Glass Eyes by Blampoix with Brevete Body Mark

28" (71 cm.) Porcelain shoulder head with delicately pink tinted complexion, rounded facial shape, slightly elongated throat, almond shaped brown glass enamel inset eyes, thick dark eyeliner, lightly feathered brows, accented nostrils, closed mouth with center accent line on lips, brunette human

216. French Bisque Poupée with Dehors Articulation and Wooden Body

18" (46 cm.) Bisque swivel head on kid-edged bisque shoulder plate, neck articulation that allows the doll to tilt head forward and sideways as well as swivel, almond shaped blue glass enamel inset eyes, painted lashes and brows, accented nostrils and eye corners, closed mouth with accented lips, pierced ears, brunette human hair wig over cork pate, French kid-over-wooden poupée body with shapely torso, dowel-jointing at shoulders, hips, and knees, bisque lower arms, wearing antique black taffeta gown and bonnet, undergarments. Condition: generally excellent, rub on under chin, both thumbs missing. Marks: 4. Comments: attributed to Dehors who deposed the realistic neck articulation in 1867. Value Points: lovely lady with rare articulation and wooden body. $3000/4000

217. Large French Bisque Poupée in the Barrois Manner with Crimean War Costume

32" (81 cm.) Bisque swivel head on kid-edged bisque shoulder plate, plump facial modeling with defined double chin, almond shaped blue glass enamel inset eyes, dark eyeliner, painted lashes, arched feathered brows, accented nostrils and eye corners, closed mouth, accented lips, pierced ears, brunette human hair wig over cork pate, French kid poupée body with shapely torso, gusset-jointing of limbs, stitched and separated fingers and toes. Condition: generally excellent. Comments: attributed to Barrois, circa 1865, the doll depicts a Crimean War Nurse, romanticized in the public eye by the pioneering nursing efforts of Florence Nightingale. Value Points: beautiful bisque and painting on the large early poupée with original nurse's uniform comprising blue and white striped uniform, undergarments, apron and cap with red cross emblem, shoes, and wonderful blue woolen cape with red woolen lining. $6000/8000

218. Rare German Bisque Character "Vanta Baby" by Amberg

23" (58 cm.) Solid domed bisque socket head, sculpted brown baby hair with modeling detail at forehead crown, narrow blue glass sleep eyes, painted lashes, lightly tinted brows, open mouth, shaded and outlined lips, two porcelain upper teeth, tongue, composition bent limb baby body, wearing peach organdy baby dress and bonnet. Condition: generally excellent. Marks: Vanta Baby L.A. & S. DRGM made in Germany. Comments: Amberg, circa 1927, the doll was commissioned by the American importer as a promotional piece for Vanta baby costumes, and was available in 5 sizes according to the 1927 advertisement in Playthings. Value Points: rare character with unique expression, beautiful bisque quality. $900/1300

219. Rare German Bisque Mechanical Musical Character, 980, by Marseille

27" (69 cm.) Bisque socket head with very plump cheeks and chin, blue glass eyes, dark eyeliner, painted curly lashes, short brush-stroked brows, accented eye corners and nostrils, open mouth, shaded and outlined lips, two porcelain upper teeth, tongue, blonde mohair wig, composition bent limb baby body, antique peach linen dress with embroidery, lace bonnet. Condition: generally excellent. Marks: A 980 M Germany 16 DRGM. Comments: Marseille, circa 1920, with hidden music box in torso, and clockwork mechanism that causes the baby to create four amusing activites: turning head side to side, arms waving, eyes moving from side to side as though following an activity, while

he licks his tongue from side to side. Value Points: very rare and delightful character whose antic movements are complemented by facial expression and beautiful bisque, original body and body finish, great larger size. $2000/3000

220. German Bisque Toddler, 10532, by Gebruder Heubach

13" (33 cm.) Bisque socket head, blue glass sleep eyes, painted lashes, feathered brows, accented nostrils and eye corners, open mouth, accented lips, row of porcelain teeth, blonde mohair wig, composition five piece toddler body, antique cotton romper suit with embroidered details. Condition: generally excellent. Marks: 10532 Heubach (square) Germany 5. Comments: Gebruder Heubach, circa 1920. Value Points: appealing worried expression on the rarely found little toddler, excellent quality of bisque. $1100/1500

221. Very Rare German Bisque Toddler, 10617, by Gebruder Heubach

25" (64 cm.) Bisque socket head with rounded facial shape, plump cheeks, blue glass sleep eyes, painted curly lashes, incised eyeliner, short feathered brows, accented eye corners, shaded nostrils, open mouth, shaded and outlined lips, two porcelain teeth, tongue, dimpled chin and cheek corners, brunette mohair wig, composition five piece toddler body with side-hip jointing, antique pinafore dress, blouse, undergarments, leather slippers. Condition: generally excellent. Marks: 10617 Heubach (square) Germany 13. Comments: Gebruder Heubach, circa 1918. Value Points: extremely rare model, previously undocumented, in fine large size with very expressive features, choice bisque and sculpting. $3500/4500

222. German Bisque Mechanical Walking Doll by Gebruder Heubach

6" (15 cm.) Solid domed bisque socket head with painted blonde boyish hair, intaglio blue side-glancing eyes, single stroke brows, closed mouth modeled as though open with laughing expression, two beaded lower teeth, carton torso, wire upper arms and legs, metal feet. When keywound, the little doll totters from side to side as though learning to walk. Condition: generally excellent. Marks: Heubach (square mark). Comments: Gebruder Heubach, circa 1920. Value Points: amusing little doll whose eager and delighted expression matches his activity. $700/900

224. Petite French Bisque Bébé Jumeau, Size 3

12" (30 cm.) Bisque socket head, blue glass paperweight inset eyes, lushly painted lashes, blue glass paperweight inset eyes, brush-stroked and multi-feathered brows, accented nostrils, closed mouth with outlined lips, pierced ears, blonde mohair wig over cork pate, French composition and wooden fully-jointed body, silk costume, undergarments, bonnet, stockings, shoes. Condition: generally excellent. Marks: Depose Tete Jumeau Bte SGDG 3 (head) Jumeau Medaille d'Or Paris (body). Comments: Emile Jumeau, circa 1886. Value Points: pretty petite bébé has dramatic large eyes, lovely bisque. $3000/4000

223. Beautiful Large French Bisque Bébé Jumeau, Size 15, with Luminous Bisque

32" (81 cm.) Bisque socket head, large amber brown glass paperweight inset eyes, dark eyeliner, lushly painted lashes, brush-stroked and multi-feathered brows with enhancing decorative glaze, accented nostrils and eye corners, closed mouth with defined space between the shaded and outlined lips, separately modeled pierced ears, French composition and wooden fully-jointed body, lovely antique lace dress, undergarments, silk bonnet. Condition: generally excellent. Marks: Depose Tete Jumeau Bte SGDG 15 (head) Jumeau Medaille d'Or Paris (body). Comments: Emile Jumeau, circa 1886. Value Points: beautiful and rare large size closed mouth bébé has gorgeous bisque, original body and body finish, original signed Jumeau shoes. $6500/8500

225. French Bisque Automaton "Dancer with Tambourine" by Vichy

20" (51 cm.) Posed upon a flat red-velvet covered platform is a bisque-headed doll with blue glass paperweight eyes, painted dark curly lashes, brush-stroked and feathered brows, accented nostrils, rose blushed eye shadow, closed mouth, accented lips, pierced ears, brunette human hair over cork pate, bisque shoulder plate and lower arms, carton torso that contains clockwork mechanism, carton legs, one posed with pointing toe, the other with bent knee and foot in air. When wound the doll pirouettes, periodically kicks foot, moves head in realistic manner, and shakes the tambourine she holds in her left hand, music plays. Condition: generally excellent, mechanism and music function well. Comments: Gustav Vichy, circa 1885. Value Points: the rare automaton wears her original Moroccan silk costume with decorative jewelry and beads, has most appealing movements, two tunes with original paper tune label indicating "Polka du Colonel" and "Les Yeux Bleu Valse". $6000/8500

Detail 226.

226. Rare French Bisque Two-Faced Character by Emile Jumeau

18" (46 cm.) Bisque socket head with two faces designed that one face be shown while the other is hidden, and then reversed at will. One face depicts a crying child with very narrow blue glass inset eyes, painted lashes, brush-stroked and feathered brows, shaded nostrils, eye corners, closed mouth modeled as though open in crying expression, modeled tongue and row of beaded teeth, crystal tear; the alternate face depicts a child with laughing expression, blue glass paperweight eyes, lushly painted lashes, brush-stroked and feathered brows, accented nostrils and eye corners, closed mouth with beaming smile, accented lips, two rows of beaded teeth. The head is enclosed in a paper mache hood with turning loop at the crown, and attached to French composition and wooden fully-jointed body. Condition: generally excellent. Marks: 7. Comments: Emile Jumeau, circa 1895, models 203 and 211 from his art character series. Value Points: rare and highly characterized faces with beautiful bisque, crystal tear, original body, silk dress, antique bonnet and Jumeau shoes. $12,000/16,000

227. French Bisque Bébé E.J. by Jumeau, Size 7

16" (41 cm.) Pressed bisque socket head, brown glass paperweight inset eyes, lushly painted lashes, rose blushed eye shadow, brush-stroked and feathered brows, accented nostrils and eye corners, closed mouth with center accent line, pierced ears, brunette human hair wig over cork pate, French composition and wooden fully-jointed body with straight wrists, nicely costumed in black velvet and burgundy silk dress, undergarments, silk bonnet, bébé pin, shoes, socks. Condition: very faint hairline high on forehead, otherwise excellent. Marks: Depose E 7 J. Comments: Emile Jumeau, circa 1885. Value Points: very pretty cabinet size bébé with beautiful decoration of eyes. $3000/3500

228. Very Lovely French Bisque Premiere Bébé by Jumeau

14" (36 cm.) Pressed bisque socket head, brown glass enamel inset eyes of great depth, dark upper eyeliner, painted lashes, mauve blushed eye shadow, lightly feathered brows, accented eye corners, shaded nostrils, closed mouth with defined space between the outlined lips, pierced ears, blonde mohair wig over cork pate, French composition and wooden eight-loose-ball-jointed body with straight wrists, nicely costumed in maroon woolen dress with velvet and silk trim, matching bonnet, undergarments, leather shoes. Condition: generally excellent. Marks: 5 (head) Jumeau Medaille d'Or Paris (body). Comments: Emile Jumeau, circa 1878, the earliest model bébé referred to as "premiere". Value Points: gorgeous early bébé with superior bisque and painting, original body and body finish, lovely antique costume. $6000/8000

229. Two Antique Silk Costumes for Costuming Large Dolls

Suitable for costuming large dolls about 35"-40". Comprising ivory silk dress with smocking at the yoke, poufy sleeves, and rows of tucking at the hem; along with ivory silk satin padded and lined coat with lace edging on the collar and fine silk thread embroidery. Excellent condition. Late 19th century. $400/500

230. Four Antique Doll Bonnets

In a variety of sizes, for bébés or poupée. Of white heavily starched cottons with elaborate cutwork border, laces, creamy cashmere with rope trim, one with original London milliner label. Excellent condition. Mid/late 19th century. $400/600

231. Gorgeous French Bisque Portrait Bébé by Jumeau with Fabulous Costume

22" (56 cm.) Pressed bisque socket head, brown glass enamel inset eyes, dark eyeliner, delicately painted lashes, lightly feathered brows, mauve blushed eye shadow, accented eye corners, shaded nostrils, closed mouth, defined space between the shaded and outlined lips, pierced ears, blonde mohair wig, cork pate, French composition and wooden eight loose-ball-jointed body with straight wrists. Condition: generally excellent. Marks: Jumeau Medaille d'Or Paris (body). Comments: Emile Jumeau, earliest period bébé known as "portrait" in reference to its luxury production, having superb bisque and well-defined features, original body and body finish, wearing fine antique rose silk costume, leather shoes with rosettes and impressed boutique label. $7500/9500

232. German Bisque Child, 171, by Kestner with Mint Excelsior Body

32" (81 cm.) Bisque socket head, brown glass sleep eyes, painted lower lashes, slightly modeled brows with brush-stroked detail and decorative glaze, accented nostrils and eye corners, open mouth, shaded and outlined lips, four porcelain teeth, brunette human hair over porcelain pate, composition and wooden ball-jointed body, antique dress included. Condition: generally excellent. Marks: M 1/2 made in Germany 16 1/2 171 (head) Excelsior Germany (red stamp on torso). Comments: Kestner, circa 1900. Value Points: beautiful child doll with superb bisque, original body and body finish. $800/1000

233. All-Original German Bisque Child, 146, by Kestner with Excelsior Body

33" (84 cm.) Bisque socket head, brown glass sleep eyes, dark painted curly lashes, thick dark eyeliner, brush-stroked and feathered brows with decorative glaze, accented eye corners, shaded nostrils, open mouth, shaded and outlined lips, four porcelain teeth, dimpled chin, brunette human hair over plaster pate, composition and wooden ball-jointed body. Condition: generally excellent. Marks: N made in Germany 17 146 (head) Excelsior Germany (body). Comments: Kestner, circa 1900. Value Points: beautiful child in fine large size with lovely bisque and mint signed original body. $800/1000

234. Large Early 20th Century Mannequin Child with Bisque Head by Kestner

44" (112 cm.) Bisque socket head, grey glass eyes, painted lashes, brush-stroked brows, accented nostrils and eye corners, open mouth, accented lips, four porcelain teeth, on black muslin covered mannequin body, wooden arms with dowel articulation at shoulders, elbows and wrists, hand-carved wooden hands, cast iron feet with sculpted boots. Condition: generally excellent, hands may not be original. Marks: 0 1/2 made in Germany 18 1/2. Comments: Kestner, circa 1910. Value Points: handsome mannequin with fine quality of bisque, articulated arms. $1200/1700

235. German All-Bisque Child, 200, by Kestner

9" (23 cm.) One piece bisque head and torso, blue glass sleep eyes, painted lashes, feathered brows, accented nostrils, open mouth, slightly parted lips, row of tiny teeth, accented lips, brunette mohair wig, loop-jointed bisque arms and legs, painted white ribbed stockings with blue rims, black one-strap heeled shoes, nicely costumed. Condition: hairlines on torso and right leg. Marks: 83/200 22. Comments: Kestner, circa 1920. Value Points: great large size all-bisque with expressive features. $300/500

236. German Bisque Child, 142, by Kestner with Excelsior Body

36" (91 cm.) Bisque socket head, blue glass sleep eyes, painted lashes, brush-stroked brows with sculpting detail, accented nostrils, open mouth, shaded and accented lips, four porcelain teeth, brunette mohair wig over plaster pate, composition and wooden ball-jointed body. Condition: generally excellent. Marks: 0 1/2 made in Germany 18 1/2 142 (head) Excelsior Germany 9 (body). Comments: Kestner, circa 1900. Value Points: beautiful Kestner child with signed deluxe model body, choice bisque, original wig, multi-layered antique costume. $900/1200

generally excellent. Marks: F made in Germany 10 247 JDK 10. Comments: Kestner, circa 1914. Value Points: endearing child with impressed dimples, lovely bisque, original body, wig, body finish. $700/1000

239. German All-Bisque "Bye-Lo Baby" with Original Paper Label

8" (20 cm.) One piece bisque head and torso, solid domed head with brown tinted baby hair, painted facial features, small blue eyes, tinted brows, broad nose with accented nostrils, closed mouth with center accent line, loop-jointed bisque arms and legs with bare feet. Condition: generally excellent. Marks: 20-20 (torso). Marks: Bye-lo Baby Made in Germany (paper label). Comments: circa 1923. Value Points: large size of the all-bisque with original paper label. $400/500

240. Exceptionally Large German Bisque Character, 260, by Kestner with Flirty Eyes

42" (107 cm.) Bisque socket head, brown glass sleep and flirty eyes, dark painted eyeliner, painted curly lashes, brush-stroked brows, mohair lashes, open mouth, painted and accented lips, four porcelain teeth, tongue, brunette human hair wig, composition and wooden ball-jointed body. Condition: generally excellent. Marks: made in Germany JDK 260. Comments: Kestner, circa 1914. Value Points: largest size of the delightful character, beautiful bisque, flirty eyes, antique whitewear costume. $2000/2500

237. German Bisque Toddler, 247, by Kestner Known as "Baby Jean"

19" (48 cm.) Bisque socket head, blue glass sleep eyes, dark eyeliner, painted curly lashes, short feathered brows, accented nostrils and eye corners, open mouth, outlined lips, two porcelain upper teeth, impressed cheek and chin dimples, blonde mohair wig over plaster pate, composition and wooden ball-jointed toddler body with side-hip jointing, antique costume. Condition: generally excellent. Marks: H made in Germany 12 247 JDK. Comments: Kestner, circa 1915. Value Points: delightful toddler with wonderful impressed dimples, original wig, pate, body, body finish. $800/1200

238. German Bisque Character "Baby Jean", 247, by Kestner

13" (33 cm.) Bisque socket head, blue glass sleep eyes, painted lashes, feathered brows, accented nostrils and eye corners, open mouth, outlined lips, two porcelain upper teeth, tongue, brunette mohair bobbed wig, composition bent limb baby body, antique costume. Condition:

241. German Bisque Character, 260, by Kestner with Extended Length Original Wig

34" (86 cm.) Bisque socket head, blue glass sleep eyes, painted dark curly lashes, brush-stroked and multi-feathered brows, accented nostrils, open mouth, outlined lips, four porcelain teeth, brunette mohair wig, composition and wooden ball-jointed body. Condition: generally excellent. Marks: made in Germany JDK 260 92. Comments: Kestner, circa 1915. Value Points: beautiful original condition with superb elongated soft mohair wig, wonderful antique cutwork white cotton dress, undergarments, stockings, shoes. $1200/1800

242. German Bisque Toddler, 260, by Kestner with Flirty Eyes

18" (46 cm.) Bisque socket head, large brown glass "flirty" eyes, dark painted eye liner, painted curly lashes, short feathered and "fly-away" brows, accented nostrils and eye corners, open mouth, outlined lips, four porcelain teeth, brunette mohair wig, composition and wooden ball-jointed toddler body with side-hip jointing, antique costume. Condition: generally excellent. Marks: made in German JDK 260 48. Comments: Kestner, circa 1915. Value Points: very beautiful lustrous patina on the wide-eyed urchin with original toddler body. $700/900

243. Sonneberg Bisque Child, 137, by Mystery Maker with Beautiful Eyes

23" (58 cm.) Bisque socket head with flattened solid dome, large blue glass inset eyes, dark painted curly lashes, thick dark eyeliner, brush-stroked and multi-feathered brows, accented eye corners, shaded nostrils, closed mouth with defined space between the shaded and outlined lips, pierced ears, blonde mohair wig, pierced ears, Sonneberg composition and wooden fully-jointed body with straight wrists, lovely antique costume and bonnet. Condition: generally excellent. Marks: 137 14. Comments: mystery maker, circa 1885. Value Points: especially beautiful closed mouth doll with entrancing large eyes. $2200/2800

244. Sonneberg Bisque Child with Expressive Face

13" (33 cm.) Bisque swivel head on kid-lined

bisque shoulder plate, blue glass inset eyes, dark eyeliner, painted lashes, feathered brows, rose blushed eye shadow and cheek blush, accented eye corners and nostrils, open mouth, outlined lips, double row of tiny porcelain teeth, pierced ears, blonde mohair wig, commercial kid body with stitch-jointing, bisque forearms. Condition: generally excellent, some kid wear, thumbs missing. Marks: 6. Comments: Sonneberg, circa 1885, the doll was made to compete with the French market, and closely resembles an early Jumeau bébé. Value Points: pretty child doll with swivel head, beautiful blushing, antique silk dress, undergarments, kid shoes, bonnet. $800/1000

245. German Bisque Character, 154, by Hertel and Schwab

14" (36 cm.) Solid domed bisque socket head, brown sculpted boyish hair with modeled forelock curl, sculpted ears, brown glass sleep eyes, long painted curly lashes, feathered brows, accented

nostrils, closed mouth with pouty expression, outlined lips, composition five piece toddler body. Condition: generally excellent. Marks: 154/4. Comments: Hertel and Schwab, circa 1912, the model known as "Tommy Tucker". Value Points: fine quality of bisque on the appealing character, wearing antique Tyrolean style costume. $1200/1800

246. Large German Bisque Closed Mouth Child by Kestner

28" (71 cm.) Bisque socket head, blue glass sleep eyes, thick dark eyeliner, painted dark curly lashes, brush-stroked and feathered brows, accented nostrils and eye corners, closed mouth, accented lips, brunette mohair wig over plaster pate, early composition and wooden body with loose-ball-jointing at shoulders and hips, straight wrists. Condition: generally excellent. Marks: Made in Germany 16. Comments: Kestner, circa 1890. Value Points: beautiful large model of the wide-eyed closed mouth child, excellent bisque, original body and body finish, elongated wig, pate, wonderful costume. $2500/3000

247. Large German Bisque Child, 142, by Kestner with Mint Excelsior Body

36" (91 cm.) Bisque socket head with elongated facial modeling, full cheeks, brown glass sleep eyes, painted lashes, thick brush-stroked brows with very full sculpted detail, accented eye corners and nostrils, open mouth, outlined lips, four porcelain teeth, brunette mohair wig over plaster pate, composition and wooden ball-jointed body. Condition: generally excellent. Marks: 0 1/2 made in Germany 18 1/2 142 (head) Excelsior Germany (body). Comments: Kestner, circa 1900. Value Points: beautiful large child has original wig, pate, luxury Excelsior body, body finish, included is antique dress and bonnet. $1200/1600

antique corset. Condition: generally excellent. Marks: 13 made in Germany 162 (head) Germany (body). Comments: Kestner, circa 1900, their composition bodied version of the Gibson Girl. Value Points: hard to find fashion lady in wonderful larger size with beautiful bisque, decorative glaze on brows and lips, original lady body with original finish. $1700/2500

249. German Bisque Child, 109, by Handwerck with John Wanamaker Store Label

24" (61 cm.) Bisque socket head, large blue glass sleep eyes, dark eyeliner, dark painted curly lashes, brush-stroked widely arched brows, accented nostrils and eye corners, open mouth, accented lips, four porcelain teeth, pierced ears, blonde mohair wig, composition and wooden ball-jointed body. Condition: generally excellent. Marks: 109 - 12 Dep Germany. Comments: Heinrich Handwerck, circa 1910. Value Points: pretty child wears her original simple muslin dress with peach silk ribbons, large hair ribbon in original wig, and has original label on torso "Finest quality, Made in Germany for John Wanamaker". $400/600

250. Two German Bisque Dolls, 1160, by Simon and Halbig, Known as "Little Women"

13" (33 cm.) largest, 6" smaller. Each has bisque shoulder head with brown glass eyes, painted lashes, feathered brows, accented nostrils, closed mouth with primly set lips, muslin body. The larger doll has pierced ears, porcelain limbs, and very elaborate original mohair wig with long ringlet curls at sides and coiled

248. German Bisque Lady Doll, 162, by Kestner with Original Lady Body

25" (64 cm.) Bisque socket head, blue glass sleep eyes, thick dark eyeliner, painted long lashes, brush-stroked and feathered brows, accented nostrils and eye corners, open mouth, outlined lips, four porcelain teeth, pierced ears, brunette human hair in upswept fashion over plaster pate, composition and wooden ball-jointed lady body with shapely bosom, waist, and derriere, elongated limbs with straight wrists, wearing pretty antique lingerie, with

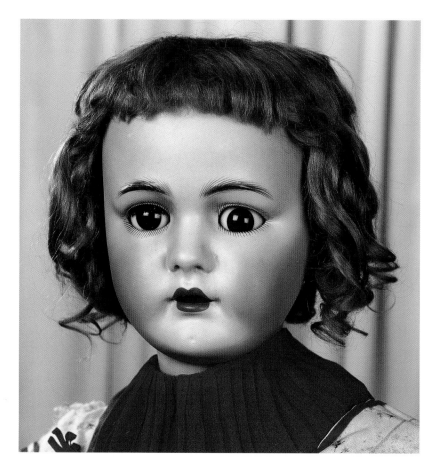

braid at the back, silk dress; the smaller has original blonde mohair wig, bisque limbs, original muslin house dress. Condition: generally excellent. Marks: S&H 1160 3 (larger) 8/0 (smaller). Comments: Simon and Halbig, circa 1890. Value Points: a delightful size comparison between largest and smallest of this model, each with fine original wig. $700/900

251. Large German Bisque Child by Kammer and Reinhardt

36" (90 cm.) Bisque socket head, brown glass sleep eyes, dark eyeliner, painted curlylashes, slightly modeled brush-stroked brows with feathered detail, accented nostrils and eye corners, open mouth, shaded and outlined lips, pierced ears, four porcelain teeth, pierced ears, brunette mohair wig, composition and wooden ball-jointed child body with side-hip jointing, lovely Kate Greenaway style antique dress, undergarments, stockings, shoes. Condition: generally excellent. Marks: K*R Simon & Halbig Germany 90. Value Points: fine large child with beautiful matte bisque, lovely decoration of eyes and lips, original body and body finish. $1600/2200

252. Large Bisque Lady Doll for the French Market with Rare Daspres "La Patricienne" Body

25" (64 cm.) Bisque socket head with slender facial shape of adult woman, brown glass sleep eyes, dark painted lashes, dark curly lashes, thick brush stroked and feathered brows, accented nostrils and eye corners, open mouth, accented lips, four porcelain teeth, pierced ears, antique hand-tied brunette human hair, composition fully-jointed lady body with unique sculpting, shapely bosom, waist and derriere, elongated limbs, large hips, hands and feet. Condition: generally excellent. Marks: S&H dep 1159 11 (head) E.D.B La Patricienne Depose (body). Comments: Edmund Daspres, successor to the Jules Steiner firm, deposed the model in 1905, with distinctive lady body shape designed to accomodate fashions of that era; the Simon and Halbig head was commissioned for this doll. Value Points: beautiful and rare large lady doll with lovely bisque and expression, wonderfully sculpted body, antique lingerie. $4000/5000

253. German Bisque Doll "Bébé Elite" by Max Handwerck in Bridegroom Costume

28" (71 cm.) Bisque socket head, brown glass sleep eyes, delicately painted lashes, lightly feathered brows, accented nostrils and eye corners, open mouth, shaded lips, four porcelain teeth, brunette wig, composition and wooden ball-jointed body. Condition: generally excellent, body repainted. Marks: Max Handwerck Bébé Elite 286/10 Germany. Comments: Max Handwerck, circa 1915. Value Points: with expressive features, the doll wears his original tailor-made bridegroom tuxedo, commissioned from tailor at a cost of $45; the doll was referred to by Carole Jean Zvonar as "the worried bridegroom". $600/800

254. Rare Large American Child's Piano by Schoenhut

25" (64 cm.) h. 23"w. An upright piano with wonderful cabinet featuring fancy heavy carved legs, faux foot pedals, separate music rack, hinged key cover, 22 keys with actual notes, is decorated with superb gilt and red stencils in elaborate scrolls and garlands, along with Schoenhut emblems and gold lettering "Schoenhut" in Germanic script. Condition: generally excellent. Comments: Schoenhut of Philadelphia, circa 1900, the piano was acquired by Carole Jean Zvonar from its original family owners in Pennsylvania. Value Points: very deluxe toy piano whose size and quality of music allowed its actual use by a young child learning to play, superb decorations are perfectly preserved. $800/1200

255. Pretty French Bisque Bébé by Rabery and Delphieu

18" (46 cm.) Bisque socket head, brown glass enamel inset eyes, painted lashes, rose blushed eye shadow, thick brush stroked and feathered brows, accented nostrils and eye corners, closed mouth with defined space between the outlined lips, pierced ears, dimpled chin, blonde mohair wig over cork pate, French composition and wooden eight-loose-ball-jointed body with straight wrists, wearing antique burgundy silk dress and bonnet with lace appliques, undergarments, stockings, cream kid shoes with original "Au Louvre" Paris department store label. Condition: generally excellent. Marks: R. 1 D. Comments: Rabery and Delphieu, circa 1885. Value Points: pretty bébé with well-painted features, original body and body finish. $3000/4000

256. French Bisque Bébé by Jules Steiner with Original Body Label

23" (58 cm.) Bisque socket head, blue glass paperweight inset eyes, dark painted eye-liner, painted lashes, brush-stroked and multi-feathered brows, accented eye corners, shaded nostrils, closed mouth with defined space between the shaded lips, pierced ears, brunette human hair hand-tied wig over cork pate, French

composition and wooden fully-jointed body, rose silk dress with Bertha collar and pouf sleeves, matching hair-bow, undergarments, leather shoes, stockings. Condition: generally excellent. Marks: J. Steiner Bte SGDG Paris Few A 15 (head) (original paper label on body). Comments: Jules Steiner, circa 1890. Value Points: pretty shy-faced bébé with lovely bisque, original body and body finish. $3000/4000

257. Pretty Petite French Bisque Bébé Steiner in Red Silk Dress

15" (38 cm.) Bisque socket head, blue glass paperweight inset eyes, painted lashes, feathered brows, accented nostrils and eye corners, closed mouth with defined space between the outlined lips, pierced ears, brunette human hair over cork pate, French composition body with jointing at shoulders and hips. Condition: generally excellent. Marks: A-7 Paris (head) Bébé Parisien Medaille d'Or Paris (body). Comments: Jules Steiner, circa 1890. Value Points: pretty petite bébé with lustrous patina on rosy cheeks, wears antique red silk dress with lace trim, matching bonnet, undergarments, stockings, leather shoes. $2500/3000

258. American Toy Wooden "Grand Piano"

11" (28 cm.) h. 15"w., 17"d. A wooden toy piano in the style of a grand piano has hinged keyboard cover, 17 working keys, and a hinged lid that can be displayed up or down. A decoupage lyre appears on the front flanked by words "Grand Piano" and "reg. U.S. Pat. office". Excellent condition. Circa 1930. $400/500

259. German All-Bisque Large Piano Baby by Hertwig

10" (25 cm.) One piece all-bisque figure of seated baby, his head tilted backward, with tousled very curly brown hair, painted facial features depicting a smiling child, intaglio eyes, row of beaded teeth, elaborately sculpted costume with beaded decorations, the baby's arms modeled away from body holding a spoon in one hand and a bowl in the other. Condition: small chip on underside of bowl, original firing line at left knee. Comments: attributed to Hertwig, circa 1910. Value Points: wonderful expression on the large piano baby with superb detail of decoration. $400/500

260. Superb French Bisque Bébé E.J. by Jumeau, Size 11, in Near Mint Condition

25" (64 cm.) Bisque socket head, blue glass paperweight inset eyes, dark eyeliner, lushly painted lashes, brush-stroked and multi-feathered brows, accented nostrils, blushed eye shadow, shaded nostrils, closed mouth with defined space between the outlined lips, separately modeled and pierced ears, brunette antique hand-tied human hair wig over cork pate, French composition and wooden eight-loose-ball-jointed body with very plump limbs. Condition: generally excellent. Marks: Depose E 11 J (head) Jumeau Medaille d'Or Paris (body). Comments: Emile Jumeau, circa 1884. Value Points: superb refined model of the signature bébé having grand size, outstanding bisque and painting, sculpting details including impressed dimples at lip corners and chin, original body and body finish, antique costume that is likely original, lace bonnet, undergarments, knit stockings, Jumeau leather shoes signed Paris Depose 11. $7500/9500

261. Beautiful German Bisque Figure "Curtseying Girl" by Gebruder Heubach

16" (41 cm.) One piece bisque figure depicting a young lady with flowing brown hair in long tousled curls, posed as though curtseying, her intaglio eyes glancing to the right, with sculpted detail of costume including Dresden like lace collar, painted flowers on gown, bows on shoes and collar. The doll is standing upon a self base against a green leaf. Condition: generally excellent, one side of pink collar bow is missing. Comments: Gebruder Heubach, circa 1890. Value Points: very beautiful detail of sculpting on the large figure. $600/800

262. German Bisque Closed Mouth Doll

24" (61 cm.) Bisque shoulder head turned slightly to the right, very plump face, blue glass enamel inset eyes, painted lashes and brows, accented eye corners and nostrils, closed mouth with center accent line, blonde mohair wig, plaster pate, commercial kid body with very elongated limbs, stitch-jointing, bisque forearms with separately sculpted fingers, lovely antique costume. Condition: bisque and body excellent, albeit slightly mis-sized for each other. Marks: 9. Comments: Germany, circa 1885. Value Points: pretty closed mouth child with well-defined features. $400/600

263. French Bisque Bébé with Distinctive Features by Joanny

22" (56 cm.) Bisque socket head with elongated facial shape, full cheeks, deep blue glass paperweight inset eyes, dark eyeliner, painted lashes, brush-stroked and feathered brows, accented eye corners, shaded nostrils, closed mouth with accented lips, pierced ears, brunette mohair wig over cork pate, French composition and wooden fully-jointed body with straight wrists. Condition: generally excellent. Marks: J 9. Comments: Joseph Joanny, circa 1885, the firm which created few dolls was located at the Rue de Rivoli in Paris during that decade. Value Points: rare doll with very expressive features, long-faced modeling, lovely bisque, fine antique costume. $5000/7500

265. German Bisque Child by Heinrich Handwerck in Original Blue Sailor Suit

31" (79 cm.) Bisque socket head, blue glass sleep eyes, painted lower lashes, mohair lashes, brush-stroked brows with comb-marked detail, decorative glaze, accented nostrils and eye corners, open mouth, accented lips, four porcelain teeth, dimpled chin, pierced ears, brunette human hair wig, composition and wooden ball-jointed body. Condition: generally excellent. Marks: Heinrich Handwerck Simon & Halbig 6 1/2 (head) Heinrich Handwerck 6 1/2 (body). Comments: very fine lustrous patina of bisque, original body and body finish, the childhood doll of Mrs. Becker of Pennsylvania, wears its original blue chambray sailor suit with red anchor trim and tie. $800/1000

266. German Bisque Child, 69, by Heinrich Handwerck with Antique Costume

25" (64 cm.) Bisque socket head, blue glass sleep eyes, dark eyeliner, painted lashes, slightly modeled brush-stroked brows, accented nostrils and eye corners, open mouth, accented lips, four porcelain teeth, dimpled chin, pierced ears, brunette human hair, composition and wooden ball-jointed body. Condition: generally excellent. Marks: 69-12x Germany Handwerck 4. Comments: Handwerck, circa 1900. Value Points: pretty dolly-face model with original body and body finish, wonderful antique costume. $600/800

264. German Bisque Child Doll by Bergmann in Original Linen Suit

29" (74 cm.) Bisque socket head, blue glass sleep eyes, dark eyeliner, painted lashes, short feathered brows, accented nostrils, open mouth, accented lips, four porcelain teeth, dimpled chin, brunette human hair bobbed wig, composition and wooden ball-jointed body. Condition: generally excellent. Marks: C.M. Bergmann Simon & Halbig 13 1/2. Comments: Bergmann, circa 1910, the doll was acquired, along with #265, from the original Becker family estate by Carole Jean Zvonar. Value Points: well-preserved condition, the doll has excellent bisque, original body finish, wears its original white linen suit. $500/700

267. Large German Bisque Toddler Character by Konig and Warnecke

25" (64 cm.) Bisque socket head, blue glass sleep eyes, painted lower lashes with dot highlights, lightly feathered curved brows, accented eye corners and nostrils, open mouth, outlined lips, two porcelain upper teeth, modeled stuck-out ears, brunette mohair bobbed wig, composition and wooden ball-jointed toddler body with side-hip jointing. Condition: generally excellent. Marks: K&W Germany 13. Comments: Konig and Warnecke, circa 1918. Value Points: fine large toddler with wonderfully sculpted featrued, very fine quality of bisque and painting, original toddler body, antique costume. $700/1000

268. Pretty German Bisque Child, 174, by Kestner

20" (51 cm.) Bisque socket head, blue glass sleep eyes, dark eyeliner, painted lashes, brush-stroked and feathered brows with decorative glaze, accented nostrils, open mouth with outlined lips, four porcelain teeth, blonde mohair wig over plaster pate, composition and wooden ball-jointed body. Condition: generally excellent. Marks: D made in Germany 8 174 (head) Germany 2 (body). Comments: Kestner, circa 1900. Value Points: pretty child has original body and body finish, wears fine antique costume. $800/1000

269. German Bisque Jubilee Googly by Hertel and Schwab

15" (38 cm.) Bisque socket head with rounded facial shape, plump cheeks, round blue glass flirty eyes, long painted curly lashes, dark eyeliner, lightly feathered brows, accented nostrils of little rounded nose, closed mouth with watermelon-slice shaped smile, shaded lips, blonde mohair fleecy wig, composition and wooden ball-jointed toddler body with side-hip jointing, antique sailor costume. Condition: generally excellent. Marks: 165 - 6. Comments: Hertel and Schwab, the model was marketed as their "Jubilee Googly", circa 1914. Value Points: delightful googly with appealing urchin expression, very fine bisque, oriignal body and body finish. $3500/4500

271. German All-Bisque Coquette by Gebruder Heubach

8" (20 cm.) One piece bisque head and torso, brown sculpted hair in curly bobbed style with painted orange headband, painted brown side-glancing eyes, single stroke brows, closed mouth with impish smile, loop-jointed bisque arms and legs, painted white bobbed socks and brown one strap shoes, antique dress. Condition: generally excellent. 3 chips on left shoulder. Comments: Gebruder Heubach, circa 1916. Value Points: cheerful imp with wonderfully modeled hair. $400/500

272. German All-Bisque Coquette by Gebruder Heubach in Smaller Size

5" (13 cm.) One piece bisque head and torso, sculpted short brown curly hair with orange headband, painted side-glancing eyes, closed mouth with impish smile, loop-jointed bisque arms, bare feet. Condition: generally excellent. Comments: Germany, circa 1920. Value Points: appealing expression and excellent bisque. $300/400

273. German All-Bisque Googly with Blue Bows

4.5" (10 cm.) One piece bisque head, torso and legs, sculpted hair with blue hair bows, painted black side-glancing googly eyes, pug nose, bow-shaped mouth, loop-jointed arms with spread fingers except 2nd and 3rd fingers modeled together, painted blue shoes, antique hanky dress. Condition: generally excellent. Comments: Gebruder Heubach, circa 1920. $300/400

270. Large German Bisque Jubilee Googly by Hertel and Schwab

25" (64 cm.) Bisque socket head with rounded facial shape, very plump cheeks, round blue glass flirty eyes, painted curly lashes, arched brows, accented nostrils and eye corners, pug nose, closed mouth with watermelon-slice-shaped smile, blushed cheeks, brunette mohair very curly wig, composition and wooden ball-jointed toddler body with side-hip jointing, antique costume. Condition: restoration around both eye rims, otherwise excellent, original body finish. Marks: 165 - 13. Comments: Hertel and Schwab, their Jubilee Googly, circa 1914. Value Points: wonderful large and rare size of the impish googly with fine quality of sculpting, original body and body finish. $4000/5500

274. Large German Bisque Two-Faced Doll by Fritz Bartenstein

19" (48 cm.) Bisque socket head with different face on either side of head, one face with blue glass enamel inset eyes, painted lashes, sculpted curvy brows to indicate frown, accented eye corners and nostrils, closed mouth modeled as though open with sculpted tongue and shaded lips, the other face with smiling expression, glass eyes, painted and feathered brows, closed mouth with upturned lips, the head enclosed in cardboard hood which forms into a shoulder plate with sculpted bodice and attaches to muslin covered torso, composition arms, nicely costumed. Condition: generally excellent. Marks: Deutsches Reichs patent U.S.P. No 243752 made in Germany. Comments: Fritz Bartenstein, circa 1892. Value Points: rarer model of the popular multi-face dolls with original signed body, working "mama" crier, antique costume. $1200/1800

275. Petite German Bisque Two-Faced Doll by Carl Bergner with Rare Black Facial Model

11" (28 cm.) Bisque socket head with two alternate faces, one having ebony black complexion with brown glass eyes, closed mouth; the other with white complexion, brown glass eyes and closed mouth. The head is enclosed in a cardpaste hood with brass knob at the top that rotates the head to reveal each face, original body with muslin over cardboard torso, composition and wooden limbs, pull-string mama crier, antique costume. Condition: generally excellent. Comments: Carl Bergner, circa 1892. Value Points: very rare model with black and white faces, beautiful sculpting and flawless painting of complexions. $1500/2000

276. German Bisque Three-Face Doll by Carl Bergner

16" (41 cm.) Bisque socket head with three alternate faces: crying with glass eyes, closed mouth and crystal tears, laughing with glass eyes and closed mouth, and sleeping with modeled closed eyelids and closed mouth. The head is enclosed within a hood that attaches to composition shoulder plate, muslin over carton torso with pull-string working "mama" crier, composition limbs, antique costume. Condition; generally excellent. Marks: C.B. (shoulder plate). Comments: Carl Bergner, circa 1892. Value Points: well detailed sculpting on the three faces. $1200/1700

Marks: AHW (in circle) Simon and Halbig Germany 156/7. Comments: Adolf Hulss, circa 1920. Value Points: rare model with rich complexion, original body and body finish, appealing expression. $800/1100

279. German Brown Bisque Child Doll with Original Costume

13" (33 cm.) Bisque socket head with light brown bisque complexion, brown glass inset eyes, black painted lashes and brows, open mouth, row of tiny teeth, brown composition and wooden fully jointed body, black fleecy mohair wig. Condition: generally excellent. Marks: 1894 AM Dep Made in Germany 3/0. Comments: Marseille, circa 1895. Value Points: pretty cabinet size doll with lustrous complexion, wears her original cotton dress and bandana, white cutwork pinafore, undergarments, stockings, shoes. $700/900

277. German Brown-Complexioned Character, 1294, by Simon and Halbig for Franz Schmidt

20" (51 cm.) Bisque socket head with brown complexion, brown glass sleep eyes, black painted curly lashes, black feathered brows, accented nostrils and eye corners, open mouth, coral shaded lips, two porcelain upper teeth, black fleecy mohair wig, brown composition bent limb baby body, antique baby dress and undergarments. Condition: generally excellent, some minor wig pulls. Marks: 1294 Simon & Halbig Made in Germany 50. Comments: Franz Schmidt, circa 1918. Value Points: sweet expression, lovely complexion with artful painting, original body and body finish. $800/1000

278. German Bisque Toddler with Brown Complexion by Adolf Hulss

16" (41 cm.) Bisque socket head with rich brown complexion, brown glass sleep eyes, black painted lashes and brows, open mouth, coral lips, two upper teeth, tongue, black fleecy mohair wig, composition five piece toddler body, antique costume with cutwork detail, bib, undergarments, shoes, socks. Condition: generally excellent, few wig pulls.

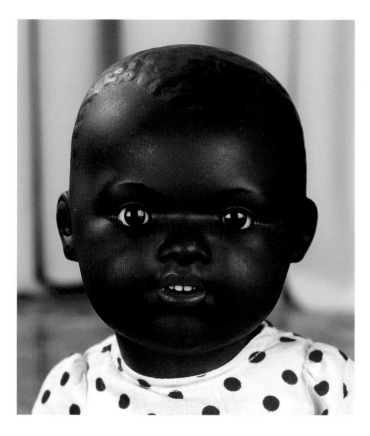

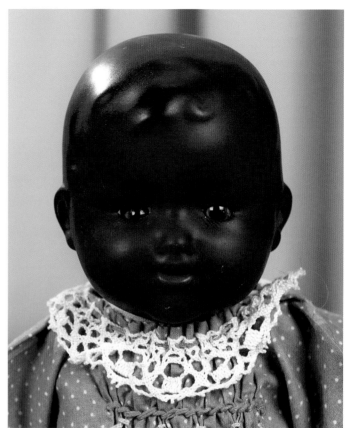

280. Rare German Brown Bisque Character, 362, by Marseille

18" (46 cm.) Bisque socket head with rich brown complexion, black sculpted tightly curled hair, brown glass sleep eyes, tinted brows, black painted lashes, open mouth, four porcelain teeth, brown composition bent limb baby body, cotton dress. Condition: generally excellent. Marks: A.M. Germany 362/6 K. Comments: Marseille, circa 1925. Value Points: rare model enhanced by superb detail of sculpting , beautiful complexion with matching body, wonderful detail of hair sculpting. $800/1200

281. German Bisque Character, 352, by Sculpted Hair and Brown Complexion

13" (33 cm.) Bisque flanged head sculpted black hair having curly details, dark chocolate brown complexion, tiny brown glass sleep eyes, black painted brows and lashes, accented nostrils, open mouth, two porcelain upper teeth, brown muslin baby body with jointing at shoulders and hips, composition hands, wearing cotton dress. Condition: generally excellent. Marks: AM Germany 352/3. Comments: Marseille, circa 1925. Value Points: rare model virtually unknown with brown complexion, has fine lustrous complexion, fine detail of sculpting. $800/1200

282. German Brown Bisque Character, "Sammy" by Marseille

14" (36 cm.) Solid domed bisque socket head with rich brown complexion, painted black hair with slight modeling detail, tinted brows, tiny brown glass sleep eyes, accented nostrils, slightly open mouth, two bottom teeth, composition bent limb baby body. Condition: generally excellent. Marks: AM Germany 351/3 x. Comments: Marseille, circa 1925. Value Points: pristine unplayed with condition, the little fellow is wearing original striped muslin chemise with original paper label "Sammy". $700/1000

284. Two German Brown Bisque Character Babies by Heubach Koppelsdorf

8" (20 cm.) Each has bisque socket head with dark brown complexion, tiny brown glass inset eyes, closed mouth with very full lips, pierced ears, brown composition bent limb baby body. Condition: generally excellent, some typical wig pulls. Marks: Heubach Koppelsdorf German (painted hair 399) (wigged 444). Comments: circa 1925. Value Points: the appealing petite pair wear matching felt skirts, bangle earrings. $600/1000

285. Rare, German Bisque Character, 463, with Brown Complexion by Heubach Koppelsdorf

7" (18 cm.) Solid domed bisque socket head, painted black hair and brows, tuft of hair at crown, brown glass side-glancing googly eyes, pierced nostrils with nose ring, slightly parted lips of beaming smile with row of painted teeth, pierced ears with bangle earrings, composition bent limb baby body. Condition: generally excellent. Marks: Heubach Koppelsdorf 463 16/0 Germany. Comments: circa 1925. Value Points: very rare model with highly characterized features, original costume and jewelry. $800/1000

283. German Black Bisque Character, 444, with Original "South Sea" Paper Label

13" (33 cm.) Bisque socket head with ebony complexion, brown glass sleep eyes, black tinted brows and lashes, accented nostrils, closed mouth with very full lips, black fleecy hair, black composition five piece toddler body. Condition: generally excellent. Marks: Heubach Koppelsdorf 444 7/0 Germany. Comments: Heubach, circa 1925. Value Points: in near mint unplayed with condition, the doll wears original grass skirt, has original label "South Seas Baby" and is preserved in base of original box with elephant illustrations. $800/1100

286. German Bisque Character, 353, by Marseille Depicting Chinese Boy

10" (25 cm.) Solid domed bisque socket head with amber brown complexion, tiny brown glass sleep eyes, black painted baby hair and brows, painted lashes, closed mouth with pensive expression, five piece toddler body. Condition: generally excellent. Marks: AM Germany 353 12/0 k. Comments: Marseille, circa 1925. Value Points: in near mint unplayed with condition, the little Chinese boy wears factory original costume and partial frail original box. $800/1200

287. German Bisque Character with Light Brown Complexion and Original Costume

11" (28 cm.) Bisque socket head with cafe-au-lait brown complexion, black painted hair and brows, tiny brown glass sleep eyes, closed mouth with pouty lips, five piece composition baby body of matching complexion. Condition: generally excellent. Marks: AM Germany 341/ K. Comments: Marseille, circa 1925. Value Points: rare complexion on the all-original, near mint exotic doll representing Burmese, with original turban, skirt, and jewelry. $700/1100

288. Large German Bisque Character, 399, with Brown Complexion by Heubach Koppelsdorf

19" (48 cm.) Bisque socket head with rich brown complexion, black painted hair and brows, small brown glass sleep eyes, broad nose, closed mouth with full lips and pouty expression, pierced ears, brown composition bent limb baby body. Condition: generally excellent. Marks: Heubach Koppelsdorf 399 3 DRGM Germany. Comments: circa 1925, the doll was acquired from a museum in Brighton, England by Carole Jean Zvonar. Value Points: exceptionally beautiful sculpting and complexion on the rare large size for this model, original body and body finish, wonderful exotic costume and necklace. $800/1200

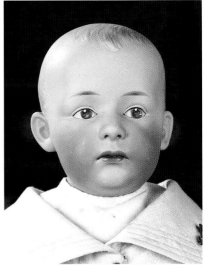

291. German Bisque Pouty Character by Gebruder Heubach

23" (58 cm.) Solid domed bisque shoulder head with pink tinted complexion, blonde painted boyish hair with modeled detail of curls, intaglio blue eyes with white eyedots, black and red upper eyeliner, brush-stroked brows, accented nostrils and eye corners, closed mouth with downcast pouty expression, muslin stitch-jointed body, bisque forearms. Condition: generally excellent. Marks: 8 Germany. Comments: Gebruder Heubach, circa 1912. Value Points: especially fine detail of sculpting on the wistful faced character. $800/1400

289. Exceptionally Large German Bisque Character, 126, by Kammer and Reinhardt with Double Row of Teeth

38" (97 cm.) Bisque socket head with rounded facial shape, blue glass sleep eyes, painted long curly lashes, brush-stroked and feathered brows, accented nostrils and eye corners, open mouth, shaded and accented lips, two porcelain upper teeth, row of smaller porcelain lower teeth, blonde mohair wig, composition and wooden ball-jointed body with plumper modeling, wearing antique dress, undergarments, stockings, shoes, hair bow. Condition: generally excellent. Marks: K*R Simon & Halbig 126 Germany. Comments: Kammer and Reinhardt, circa 1916, the largest size of their 126 model, with rare original double row of teeth only found on this size 126. Value Points: beautiful bisque and painting, with original wig and body. $1800/2400

290. German Bisque Toddler, 126, by Kammer and Reinhardt

25" (64 cm.) Bisque socket head, blue glass sleep and "flirty" eyes, painted long curly lashes, incised eyeliner, brush-stroked and feathered brows, accented nostrils and eye corners, open mouth, shaded and outlined lips, two porcelain upper teeth, tongue, brunette mohair bobbed wig, composition and wooden ball-jointed toddler body with side-hip jointing. Condition: generally excellent. Marks: K*R Simon & Halbig 126 56. Commnts: Kammer and Reinhardt, circa 1920. Value Points: the flirty eyed toddler has very fine matte bisque, original wig, body, body finish, and wearing factory original muslin romper dress with matching pants. $700/1000

292. German All-Bisque Miniature Doll

7" (18 cm.) One piece untinted bisque head and torso, painted brown hair with decorative glaze, painted blue eyes, black upper eyeliner, single stroke brows, closed mouth with little smile, pin-jointed bisque arms and legs, bare feet, costume included. Condition: generally excellent, few flakes at edges of hips. Marks: 287 (torso) 6 (legs). Comments: Germany, circa 1885. Value Points: appealing character face with smiling expression, rare brown hair. $400/600

293. German Bisque Toddler, 98, by Konig and Warnecke with Rare "Living" Eyes

21" (53 cm.) Bisque socket head, blue glass sleep eyes with extra glass layer that allows the eyes to follow from right to left in a realistic "living" manner, painted curly lashes, feathered brows, pierced nostrils, accented eye corners, open mouth, shaded and outlined lips, two porcelain upper teeth, tongue, brunette human hair, composition and wooden ball-jointed toddler body with side-hip jointing, wearing original cotton romper suit. Condition: generally excellent. Marks: made in Germany 98/10. Comments: Konig and Warnecke, circa 1920. Value Points: beautiful bisque with luminous complexion, rarer toddler body, rare "living" eyes. $900/1300

294. Rare Grand-sized German Bisque Character, 1294, by Franz Schmidt with Mechanical Eyes

29" (74 cm.) Bisque socket head, blue glass eyes that move from side to side when keywind at back of head is turned, painted long curly lashes, brush-stroked and feathered brows, accented eye corners and nostrils, open mouth, richly shaded and accented lips, two porcelain upper teeth, tongue, brunette mohair bobbed wig, composition bent limb baby body, antique costume. Condition: generally excellent. Marks: 1294 72. Comments: Simon and Halbig for Franz Schmidt, circa 1920. Value Points: rare grand size of the gentle-faced character with beautiful bisque, expressive features, enhanced by mechanical clockwork moving eyes. $1200/1800

295. Beautiful Large German Bisque Character, 1272, by Franz Schmidt

27" (69 cm.) Solid domed bisque socket head, painted blonde baby hair with defined forelock curl, modeled stuck-out ears, large blue glass sleep eyes, dark eyeliner, painted curly lashes, brush-stroked and feathered brows, open mouth, outlined lips, two beaded upper teeth, tongue, composition bent limb baby body, antique costume. Condition: generally excellent. Marks: F.S. & Co. 1272/65 Deponiert. Comments: Franz Schmidt, circa 1915. Value Points: rarer model in wonderful large size that is virtually unfindable, enhanced by very choice bisque and painting. $900/1300

296. German Bisque Character, 1271, by Franz Schmidt

13" (33 cm.) Solid domed bisque socket head, painted blonde baby hair, blue glass sleep eyes, long painted lashes, short feathered brows, accented nostrils, closed mouth modeled as though open, defined tongue tip, two beaded upper teeth, composition bent limb baby body, antique multi-layered baby costume. Condition: generally excellent. Marks: F.S. & Co 1271/35z. Comments: Franz Schmidt, circa 1916. Value Points: beautiful bisque and sculpting on the expressive character, original body and body finish, antique costume includes miniature baby rattle. $500/700

297. German Bisque Character Baby by Orsini with Laughing Expression

19" (48 cm.) l. 12" head circ. Solid domed bisque head with flanged neck, tinted tan baby hair with forelock definition, matching brows, blue glass sleep eyes, painted lashes, muslin body, composition hands, antique baby gown. Condition: generally excellent. Marks: Germany Kiddiejoy JIO c. 1926. Comments: designed by American artist, Jeannie Orsini, made in Germany, circa 1926. Value Points: rare laughing character with impressed dimples at cheeks and chin. $1100/1400

298. Pretty German Bisque Child by Bruno Schmidt in Antique Costume

25" (64 cm.) Bisque socket head, brown glass sleep eyes, painted lower lashes, short feathered brows, accented nostrils and eye corners, open mouth, outlined lips, four porcelain lips, blonde mohair wig, composition and wooden ball-jointed body. Condition: generally excellent. Marks: Made in Germany BSW (heart) 13. Comments: Bruno Schmidt, circa 1910. Value Points: Pretty rosy-cheeked child with wide eyes, original wig, well-detailed antique costume. $700/900

299. German Bisque Child, 1299, by Simon and Halbig

20" (51 cm.) Bisque socket head, brown glass sleep eyes, mohair lashes, painted lower lashes, short feathered brows, accented nostrils and eye corners, open mouth, accented lips, two porcelain upper teeth with unusual space between the teeth, brunette

Lot 298.

Lot 300.

Lot 299.

Lot 301.

mohair wig, pierced ears, composition and wooden ball-jointed body. Condition: generally excellent. Marks: 1299 Simon & Halbig S&H 7 1/2 (head) Heinrich Handwerck (body). Comments: circa 1900. Value Points: hard to find character model with unusual original teeth, impressed dimples at chin and lip corners, pull-string "mama" crier, antique aqua silk dress, undergarments, brunette mohair wig, original signed body and body finish. $700/900

300. Beautiful German Bisque Child, 192, by Kammer and Reinhardt

21" (53 cm.) Bisque socket head, brown glass sleep eyes, dark eyeliner, painted lashes, brush-stroked and feathered brows, accented nostrils and eye corners, open mouth, shaded and outlined lips, four porcelain teeth, pierced ears, blonde mohair wig, composition and wooden ball-jointed body. Condition: generally excellent. Marks: 192 1. Comments:

Kammer and Reinhardt, circa 1895. Value Points: very beautiful classic dolly-face model has lovely bisque, original wig, body, antique dress, undergarments, bonnet, wig. $800/1000

301. German Bisque Child for Carl Trautmann by Simon and Halbig

22" (56 cm.) Bisque socket head, blue glass sleep eyes, dark eyeliner, painted lashes, brush-stroked and feathered brows with decorative glaze, accented nostrils and eye corners, open mouth, accented lips, four porcelain teeth, pierced ears, brunette human hair, composition and wooden ball-jointed body, pretty antique costume. Condition: generally excellent. Marks: S&H C.T. 9. Comments: Carl Trautmann, circa 1900, the firm operated from 1884-1906 when it became Catterfelder Puppenfabrick. Value Points: rare model with lovely expression, well-modeled features, original body and body finish. $500/800

303. Large French Bisque Boy, 301, by SFBJ in Charming Costume

34" (86 cm.) Bisque socket head, blue glass sleep eyes, painted lower lashes, lightly feathered brows, accented nostrils, open mouth, outlined lips, row of small porcelain teeth, brunette human hair, French composition and wooden fully-jointed body. Condition: generally excellent. Marks: SFBJ 301 Paris 15. Comments: SFBJ, circa 1918. Value Points: the large doll wears boy's costume comprising flannel jacket, checkered pants, rebel hat,Confederate flag, corn cob pipe. $1200/1500

304. French Bisque Toddler, 236, by SFBJ in Fine Large Size

26" (66 cm.) Bisque socket head, blue glass sleep eyes, dark eyeliner, painted curly brown lashes, short feathered brows, accented nostrils and eye corners, closed mouth with laughing expression, shaded lips, modeled tongue and beaded teeth, brunette mohair bobbed wig, French composition fully-jointed toddler body with side-hip jointing, antique red cotton dress with embroidery, undergarments, red stockings, leather shoes. Condition: generally excellent. Marks: SFBJ 236 Paris 12. Comments: SFBJ, circa 1912. Value Points: especially fine quality of sculpting with well defined laughter lines and dimples, choice bisque, original wig, body, body finish. $1400/1800

305. German Bisque Crying Baby, O.I.C., by Kestner

12" (30 cm.) Solid domed bisque head with flanged neck, reddened complexion as though from crying, tinted golden baby hair and brows, tiny blue glass bead eyes, upturned nose, closed mouth modeled as though open and wailing, muslin body, celluloid hands, nicely costumed. Condition: generally

302. French Bisque Child, Size 16, with Doll Muff and Doll in Hooded Costume

35" (89 cm.) Bisque socket head, blue glass sleep eyes, mohair lashes, painted lower lashes, slightly modeled brush-stroked and feathered brows, accented nostrils and eye corners, open mouth, outlined lips, row of porcelain teeth, pierced ears, brunette human hair, French composition and wooden fully-jointed body. Condition: generally excellent. Marks: 16. Comments: SFBJ, circa 1920. Value Points: the pretty child with shy expression has original body with original finish, wears antique woolen plaid costume, undergarments, and carries her own two little toys, viz. a red mohair muff with celluloid doll head, and a small celluloid doll with red mohair hooded costume/body. $1200/1500

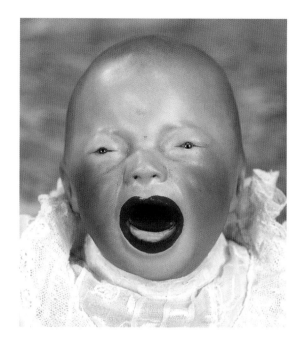

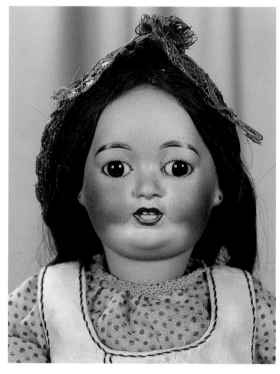

excellent. Marks: 755 3 O.I.C. Comments: Kestner, circa 1920. Value Points: rare little character with beautiful complexion that enhances the expressive features. $800/1000

306. Rare French Bisque Character "Toto" by Lanternier

18" (46 cm.) Bisque socket head, brown glass inset eyes, dark eyeliner, painted lashes, feathered brows, accented nostrils and eye corners, closed mouth modeled as though open with defined tongue tip and beaded teeth, impressed dimples, brunette human hair, French composition and wooden fully-jointed unique body. Condition: generally

excellent. Marks: Depose Toto N5 Mialone AL&Cie. Limoges. Comments: Lanternier, circa 1915. Value Points: rare character model sculpted by French artist, Mialone, for Lanternier during the art character movement of the early 20th century, delightful antic expression, lovely bisque and painting, antique costume. $1200/1700

307. French Bisque Character, 252, by SFBJ with Pouty Expression

17" (43 cm.) Bisque socket head with very full cheeks and highly defined pouty expression, blue glass sleep eyes, painted lower lashes, feathered brows, accented nostrils and eye corners, closed mouth, brunette human hair, composition five piece toddler body. Condition: generally excellent, body not original albeit of the period and appropriately sized. Marks: SFBJ 252 Paris 8. Comments: SFBJ, circa 1910, from their art character series. Value Points: petulant little character with excellent detail of sculpting, antique white pique sailor suit and cap, undergarments, shoes. $2000/3000

Kling, circa 1890. Value
Points: rare model with
expressive features, excellent
bisque, appealing petite size.
$500/700

310. French Bisque Bébé Jumeau, Size 14, with Lovely Antique Lace Dress

31" (79 cm.) Bisque socket head, brown glass paperweight inset eyes, dark painted lashes, brush-stroked and feathered brows, accented nostrils and eye corners, open mouth, outlined lips, row of porcelain teeth, pierced ears, brunette human hair, cork pate, French composition and wooden fully-jointed body. Condition: generally excellent. Marks: Tete Jumeau 14 (head) Bébé Jumeau Diplome d'honneur (body). Comments: Emile Jumeau, circa 1895. Value Points: pretty large-sized bébé has fine quality of bisque, original body and body finish, beautiful costume. $2000/3000

311. French Bisque Automata "Little Girl Knitting" by Roullet et Decamps

18" (46 cm.) Seated upon a gilded wooden chair which rests upon a red velvet covered base is a bisque-headed doll with blue glass paperweight inset eyes, painted lashes, brush-stroked and feathered brows, accented nostrils, open mouth, accented lips, row of tiny porcelain teeth, pierced ears, blonde mohair wig over cork pate, carton torso, metal upper arms and legs, paper mache lower legs posed crossed. The little girl holds knitting needles and is busily knitting a stocking; when wound music plays (two tunes) while she nods her head up and down, and

308. Rare Large German Bisque Child Doll by Kling with Bell Symbol

32" (81 cm.) Bisque socket head with elongated facial modeling, blue glass sleep eyes, dark painted lashes, brush-stroked and feathered brows, accented eye corners, shaded nostrils, open mouth, shaded and outlined lips, four porcelain teeth, brunette human hair, composition and wooden ball-jointed body. Condition: generally excellent. Marks: 370-15 K (in bell). Comments: Gebruder Kling, circa 1890. Value Points: rare large child doll by this firm, whose rarity is enhanced by beautiful expression, gorgeous bisque with luminous patina, original body and body finish, lovely antique costume. $1200/1800

309. German Bisque Child, 372, by Kling

12" (30 cm.) Bisque socket head, elongated facial modeling, brown glass sleep eyes, painted lashes and brows, accented nostrils, open mouth, accented lips, four porcelain teeth, brunette mohair wig, composition and wooden ball-jointed body, antique costume. Condition: generally excellent. Marks: Germany 372 - K (in bell). Comments:

realistically "knits". Condition: generally excellent, mechanism and music function well, costume original albeit dusty. Marks: 5 Tete Jumeau (doll). Comments: Roullet et Decamps, circa 1895. Value Points: charming automata with beautiful Jumeau head, original presentation in fancy gilded chair, and lovely accompaniment to an exhibit of small French bébés. $6000/7600

312. French Mechanical White Fur Kitten with Louis Vuitton Label

12" (30 cm.) excluding tail. A paper mache cat is lavishly covered with lush white fur, has long tail, ears, green glass eyes, pink nose, open mouth with pink lined interior, "diamond" studded silver leather necklace. When wound and lever released the cat strolls along by alternately lifting legs, and mouth opens and closes. There is a cloth label "Louis Vuitton, 70 Champs Elysees, Paris". Probably Roullet et Decamps, circa 1910. Excellent condition. $1200/1800

313. French Rosewood Toy Piano

13" (33 cm.) Wooden piano with rosewood finish has ten keys, gilded candle holders and lyre-shaped ornament, top that hinges open to reveal a sheet music and musical scales. Excellent condition. French, circa 1885. $700/900

314. Pretty German Bisque Child, 1039, by Simon and Halbig with Flirty Eyes

28" (71 cm.) Bisque socket head, blue glass sleep and flirty yes, thick dark eyeliner, painted dark lashes, brush-stroked and feathered brows, accented nostrils and eye corners, open mouth, outlined lips, four porcelain teeth, pierced ears, composition and wooden ball-jointed body, lovely antique dress. Condition: generally excellent. Marks: SH 1039 Germany dep 10. Comments: Simon & Halbig, circa 1890. Value Points: beautiful early doll with deeply defined features, lovely bisque. $1200/1600

315. German Bisque Child, 215, by Kestner with Mohair Brows

26" (66 cm.) Bisque socket head, blue glass sleep eyes, painted lashes, mohair brows in inserted slits, accented nostrils and eye corners, open

mouth, accented lips, four porcelain teeth, brunette mohair wig over plaster pate, composition and wooden ball-jointed body. Condition: generally excellent. Marks: K made in Germany 14 JDK 215 (head) Germany (body). Comments: Kestner, circa 1910. Value Points: pretty child with original body, body finish, wig, brows, pate, antique costume appears family-original. $600/900

316. Rare German Bisque Toddler by Schoneau and Hoffmeister

19" (48 cm.) Bisque socket head, blue glass sleep eyes, painted lower lashes with dot highlights, short wavy brows, accented

nostrils and eye corners, open mouth, shaded lips, two porcelain upper teeth, tongue, brunette human hair wig in long braids, composition and wooden ball-jointed toddler body with side-hip jointing, antique costume. Condition: generally excellent. Marks: S pb (in star) H B 6 Germany. Comments: Schoneau and Hoffmeister, circa 1915. Value Points: rare character model with very expressive "surprised" expression, beautiful bisque with glistening patina, original toddler body with original finish. $1100/1500

317. German Bisque Child with Rare markings and Unusual Body

22" (65 cm.) Bisque socket head, brown glass sleep eyes, thick dark eyeliner, painted lashes, brush-stroked and feathered brows, accented nostrils and eye corners, open mouth, accented lips, four porcelain teeth, pierced ears, brunette human hair, composition and wooden ball-jointed body. Condition: generally excellent. Marks: 14 1/2 N (fancy script) 6 1/2. Comments: Germany, circa 1900. Value Points: the beautiful doll has wonderful mint body with well-defined features, unusual knees, fine original finish, along with antique dress, undergarments, shoes, stockings. $800/1000

318. Large German Bisque Character Baby, 151, by Hertel and Schwab

22" (56 cm.) Solid domed bisque socket head, blonde painted baby hair with forelock curl, small blue glass sleep eyes, painted curly lashes, short feathered brows, accented nostrils, open mouth, outlined lips, modeled tongue tip, two

beaded upper teeth, composition bent limb baby body, jointed wrists. Condition: generally excellent. Marks: 151 14. Comments: Hertel and Schwab, circa 1915. Value Points: very fine detail of modeling on the large baby with original body, original body finish, unusual jointed wrists. $600/900

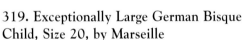

319. Exceptionally Large German Bisque Child, Size 20, by Marseille

44" (112 cm.) Bisque socket head, blue glass sleep eyes, painted lashes, thick brush-stroked brows, multi-feathered brows, accented nostrils and eye corners, open mouth, shaded and accented lips, four porcelain teeth, pierced ears, brunette mohair wig, composition and wooden ball-jointed body with unusually plump limbs and large hands, antique costume. Condition: generally excellent, some body repaint. Marks: A 20 M Germany. Comments: Marseille, circa 1915. Value Points: exceptionally large child doll with lovely bisque, the doll was a door prize at an early moving pictures theatre. $2000/2500

320. German Bisque Doll, 79, by Handwerck with Sculpted Brows in Large 42" Size

42" (107 cm.) Bisque socket head, brown glass sleep eyes, painted lashes, brush-stroked brows, accented nostrils and eye corners, open mouth, accented lips, four porcelain teeth, pierced ears, brunette human hair, composition and wooden ball-jointed body, wearing formal-wear gentleman's costume. Condition: generally excellent. Marks: 79 Germany Handwerck 4 (head) Handwerck Germany (body) Comments: Handwerck, circa 1900. Value Points: the exceptionally large size allows full beautiful expression of sculpting, bisque and painting. $2200/2800

321. Very Rare Exceptionally Large German Bisque "Walkure" by Kley and Hahn

42" (107 cm.) Bisque socket head, brown glass sleep eyes, dark painted lashes and eyeliner, accented eye corners and nostrils, open mouth, shaded lips, four porcelain teeth, pierced ears, brunette human hair, composition and wooden ball-jointed body, antique costume. Condition: generally excellent. Marks: 20 1/2 Walkure Germany 19. Comments: Kley and Hahn, circa 1900. Value Points: very rare to find this model in very large size, beautiful bisque and painting. $2500/3000

322. Rare Grand-Sized American Bisque Child by Fulper

40" (102 cm.) Pale bisque socket head, blue glass sleep eyes, painted dark lashes and brows, accented nostrils and eye corners, open mouth, accented lips, row of porcelain teeth, pierced ears, blonde human hair, composition and wooden ball-jointed body, lovely antique costume. Condition: generally excellent. Marks: CMS (intertwined in triangle) Fulper Amberg Dolls the world's Standard (incised). Comments: Fulper, New Jersey, circa 1917, the CMS initals refer to Charles Martin Stangl who headed the Fulper factory mostly know for its dinnerware; the factory produced dolls during the WWI hiatus on German dolls. Value Points: rare exceptionally large doll, believed to be the largest of this firm. $1500/2000

323. Fancy Victorian Walnut Doll's Bed with Very High Headboard

32" (81 cm.) l. 26"h. headboard. A fancy walnut doll's bed with very elaborate carving has unusually high headboard and curved footboard, with original sides, and fitted with antique linens and pieced country quilt. Condition: generally excellent. Comment: American, circa 1880. Value Points: an unusual larger size for doll play with exceptional quality of carving. $600/900

324. German Bisque Character, 525, by Kley and Hahn

12" (30 cm.) Solid domed bisque socket head, brown glass sleep eyes, painted curly lashes, lightly feathered brows, accented nostrils and eye corners, closed mouth modeled as though open, outlined lips, blonde painted baby hair, composition bent limb baby body, antique costume and saddle shoes. Condition: generally excellent, tiniest pinflake at bottom of each eye. Marks: 4 Germany K&H (in banner) 525. Comments: Kley and Hahn, circa 1915. Value Points: very fine detail of modeling, original body and body finish. $500/600

325. German Bisque Child by Wiesenthal, Schindel and Kallenberg with Original Chemise and Label

23" (58 cm.) Bisque socket head, blue glass sleep eyes, dark eyeliner, painted lashes, feathered brows, accented nostrils and eye corners, open mouth, outlined lips, four porcelain teeth, pierced ears, original blonde human hair hand-tied wig. Condition: generally excellent. Marks: Simon & Halbig WSK 4 1/2 (head). Comments: Wiesenthal, Schindel and Kallenberg, circa 1900. Value Points: the pretty child is in unplayed with condition, wearing her original muslin chemise with paper label "My Dearie WSK". $800/1000

326. Large German Bisque Child by Heinrich Handwerck in Lace Costume

33" (84 cm.) Bisque socket head, blue glass sleep eyes, painted lower lashes, slightly modeled brush-stroked brows with comb-marked details, accented eye corners and nostrils, open mouth, outlined lips, four porcelain teeth, pierced ears, blonde mohair wig, composition and wooden ball-jointed body. Condition: generally excellent. Marks: Germany Heinrich Handwerck Simon & halbig 7 (head) Handwerck (body). Comments: Handwerck, circa 1900. Value Points: large child has lovely bisque, original wig, body, body finish, beautiful lace dress that appears original, working "mama" crier. $800/1100

327. Very Large German Bisque Character, 117n, by Kammer and Reinnhardt

36" (91 cm.) Bisque socket head, blue glass sleep eyes, long curly painted lashes, slightly modeled feathered brows, accented nostrils and eye corners, open mouth, shaded and accented lips, four porcelain teeth, fine matte bisque, brunette human hair antique wig, composition and wooden ball-jointed body with above-the-knee leg jointing. Condition: generally excellent, upper legs repainted. Marks: K*R Simon & Halbig 117n Germany 90 (back of head) 30.XI.27 (crown rim). Comments: Kammer and Reinhardt, their "n" version of the 117, circa 1915. Value Points: wonderful large size of the bright-eyed child with very expressive features, original body, wearing brown silk coat with matching velvet bonnet, white cotton dress, undergarments, shoes, stockings. $1500/2500

328. Large Victorian Wicker Carriage "The Heywood" from Henry E.I. Dupont Estate

46" (117 cm.) Large and very fancily woven baby carriage with four wooden spoked wheels and curved handle, with (replaced) blue upholstery. Condition: generally excellent. Marks: The Heywood (label). Comments: Heywood Wakefield, circa 1890. Value Points: rare signed carriage in beautiful condition, from the estate of Mrs. Henry E.I. Dupont. $700/1000

329. Fancy French Bent Wire Doll Carriage

19" (48 cm.) A very fancy doll carriage is constructed of spiral woven wire in wonderful designs, has four metal spoked wheels and metal hand bar. Excellent condition. French, circa 1890. Rare design in wonderful size. $400/600

330. French Bisque Bébé Gigoteur by Jules Steiner with Au Nain Bleu Label

19" (48 cm.) Solid domed bisque head with flat-cut neck socket, brown glass enamel inset eyes, painted lashes, umber blushed eye shadow, brush-stroked brows, accented nostrils and eye corners, open mouth, shaded lips, row of tiny teeth, pierced ears, brunette mohair wig, carton torso with clockwork mechanism, composition upper arms, kid over metal upper legs, paper mache legs. When keywound and lever released, the doll cries, kicks, and waves arms. Condition: generally excellent, mechanism functions well. Marks: (Au Nain Bleu paper label on torso). Comments: Jules Steiner, the bébé marketed as "Gigoteur" was offered at the luxury Parisian toy store Au Nain Bleu, circa 1890. Value Points: pretty bébé, antique costume, boutique label, functions well. $1800/2500

Kammer and Reinhardt made dolls in a full range of sizes. Shown here, left to right, are their dolls in the following centimeter sizes: 112, 100, 90, 80 and 53. Although you imagine the smallest to be very small, it is actually nearly 2 feet tall, and the tallest doll, the boy, stands 44" or about 3 ½ feet.

Size Does Matter

Just how rare are very large dolls?
It turns out that in the matter of dolls, size does matter.

By Florence Theriault

One discerning French doll collector limits his dolls to less than 11". A knowledgeable collector in the Philippines buys only dolls that are exactly 15"; he collects every genre from gorgeous early bisque to mint hard plastic child dolls, but only those of 15". And there are books about mignonettes, and extensive research about the classic 45 centimeter French poupées.

But what about big dolls? No, not just bigger dolls, but *really* big dolls, dolls measuring more than 38" tall – that's more than 3 feet, and, in fact, just about the height of a 4 year old girl. Because so few collections have focused on grand-sized dolls, it is difficult to study them as a group. There is, however, one collector who for decades and decades has made the pursuit of very large dolls her particular passion. That is Dr. Carole Jean Zvonar of Salisbury, North Carolina, and

when her collection is explored, it becomes obvious that in the matter of dolls, size does matter. Included in the collection are a number of French and German dolls that are more than 38" tall, some ranging up to 44". Some would say this is not a large number, considering the number of years Dr. Zvonar has sought grand-sized dolls and considering her vast network of collecting friends who knew what she was seeking. She explains "Well, of course, I *was* always fussy in my choices because I only wanted perfect dolls", but then trails off with a thoughtful look and adds, "Still, wouldn't you think I could have found more?"

Her provocative question sends the curious on a search of historical doll documents, scouring for references to grand-sized dolls. Nothing. Manufacturers' catalogs make virtually no mention of super-sized dolls, a study of hundreds of vintage photographs of late 19th century trade shows and toy stores exhibits no sign of these dolls, and holiday catalogs of department and toy stores throughout France, Germany, England and America offer none of these commanding size dolls, either. The largest dolls offered in these store catalogs, in fact, are 26". And, finally, a scanning of innumerable antique doll auction catalogs for dozens of years emphasizes the fact: these dolls are scarce!

Sheer size may explain some of this rarity. An ongoing discussion in doll history concerns whether the grand-sized dolls were created for child play, as mannequins, or as decorative display pieces. Probably, it was a bit of each. Just as Dad chose the most intricate train set for Sonny but also to show off to his own friends, it is likely that sometimes large dolls were also chosen as a status symbol. If Edwina next door had a gorgeous French doll with silk costumes, "well, just look at our Martha's doll, it's twice the size", is the way that rationale probably went. The fact that grand-sized dolls seem to have only been special order dolls would enhance their boasting status even more, and the fact that the doll was really too large for Martha's playtime was really not a problem since the doll was likely only for show, anyway. As a side note, this special commission status also helps explain why grand-sized dolls seem to be of exemplary quality and luxury production.

The use of grand-sized dolls as mannequins or in decorative store displays is also well documented. Included in Dr. Carole Jean Zvonar's collection is the bisque "Vanta Baby" produced for Amberg about 1927, and specifically designed to be displayed in a children's clothing store wearing Vanta-

The little toddler standing on a chair is 15", a neat size for child play. The largest doll stands 31", a rare large size for the toddler body genre. No wonder he was used as a display doll in a Barcelona toy store for nearly a half century! (#1 and #2 in the catalog)

When a little 14" doll is set next to her grand-sized sisters, their largeness becomes apparent. All are Heinrich Handwerck dolls, model 79.

brand baby clothes. Another example is a 42" doll, by Kestner, wearing a tailor-made uniform of a Philadelphia fireman complete with silver buttons embossed "F.D. City of Philadelphia", circa 1900. The doll was displayed in the window of a prominent Philadelphia tailor, wearing this uniform, for a number of years, clearly a model for the style and quality of tailoring performed in that workshop. Carole Jean also tells the following story. "When I went to New York in 1954 to study piano at the age of 18, I saw 2 or 3 really big dolls in a Christmas scene in a Lord &Taylor store window. They were posed under a big tree just like kids opening presents. I went inside and asked and a woman told me the store had bought them in 1890 or about then for window decorations at Christmas every year".

Formen der für Amerika bestimmten Riesenpuppen

About the turn of the century German doll companies came up with an ingenious way of showing just how large "large" really was. In this antique photograph, a factory worker poses alongside body molds and body parts for grand-sized dolls which were, as the original explains, headed to the American market. (Courtesy, private archives of Marianne and Jurgen Cieslik)

Without actually being in the presence of grand-sized dolls it is difficult to convey their size. Here, the WWI Doughboy stands 30", sizeable in itself, yet dwarfed by the proximity of his 42" friend. (#30 and #31 in the catalog)

Marianne and Jurgen Cieslik, currently researching and writing a new edition of the *German Doll Encyclopedia*, corroborate the notion of very large dolls as display pieces. They write, *"Giant dolls were made in the Walterhausen area for the American market. Big chain stores used them as eye catchers. The biggest example we know was made by Simon & Halbig, marked 19, about 45" tall, the size of a 5 year old girl."* The collection of Dr. Carole Jean Zvonar includes several size 18, 40" Simon and Halbig dolls in various models, and two 42" Simon and Halbig dolls that are curiously marked with the size number 9 rather than 19.

Given their cost as well as their special order status, it is understandable that grand-size dolls are rare. Carole Jean's collection includes a 44", size 20, child doll by Marseille that was won by its original owner as a door prize at an early movie theatre. A 1925 price list for Marseille child dolls notes the following costs: size 10 at 7.50 marks, size 15 at 17.25 marks and size 20 at 34.50 marks; the size 20 was five times the cost of a doll exactly half its size! In 1924 a 50 cm child doll by K*R cost 6.60 marks wholesale and a 70 cm doll cost 12.60 marks while a 100 cm doll cost a whopping 32.50 marks! The 100 cm size

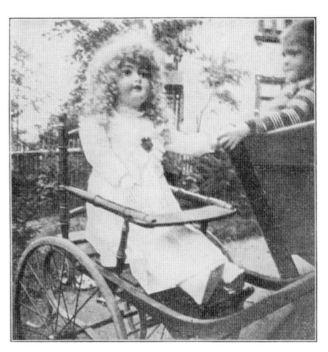

Riesenpuppe; daneben ein fünfjähriges Kind

German doll makers tried to convey the grand size of their largest doll by placing it alongside an actual 5 year old girl, as shown in this vintage photograph, circa 1910. (Courtesy, private archives of Marianne and Jurgen Cieslik)

doll was an astonishing five times the cost of a doll exactly half its size. Not twice as much, not three times as much, but five times the cost.

And, then, consider this: although the 100 cm size was the largest model offered in the K*R 1924 wholesale catalog, the collection of Carole Jean Zvonar includes two examples of the extremely rare open-mouth K*R 117 each measuring an extraordinary 112 cm (44"). Just how extra-ordinarily costly could these dolls, indubitably special commission, have been? It's no wonder they are rare.

One of the rarest dolls to appear at auction in recent years is from the Carole Jean Zvonar collection and it surely fits the category of grand-size. It was, in fact, named "Riesenbaby" which translates to "Giant Baby", when it was introduced with great fanfare by Kley and Hahn in 1912. The baby doll measures an extraordinary 37" and, remember, this is a baby body, not a child body. The head is 26" circumference, and 11" height. The waist is a gut-sucking 30" and the baby's hips, on its custom-made body, measure an astounding 27" above the hips or 34" including the legs.

The extraordinary "Riesenbaby" was actually deposed in the German courts in 1912, cited as model 571 and designated with the name "Riesenbaby" (Giant Baby) in the proceedings. It was the last model number registered by Kley and Hahn. The doll appeared in their 1912 advertising, the same year as that firm introduced their complete line of "new" standard size babies, and likely the Riesenbaby was intended as a promotional magnet for the more realistically sized dolls. Regardless of intentions, however, it is certain that the Riesenbaby was extremely limited in its production. The Cieslik's note that the "Riesenbaby is rare!" and they "have never seen another". It is likely that this doll is unique, created only for exhibition at the 1912 Leipzig Trade Fair, and that no other K&H 571 doll was ever made. Just five years shy of its 100th birthday, the doll may be one of the rarest in the world.

It really is not so difficult to figure out why the grand-sized dolls were so expensive. Consider that not only must special molds be made for the head, but also for the body. Eyes would need to be custom blown and sized, wigs with their costly mohair would require more than twice the materials of standard 24" dolls, as would costumes. Because the dolls would certainly be subject to special scrutiny by their affluent buyers, only the most skilled of the painters would be employed in their creation (which may also explain why each is so beautifully painted). And in the *German Doll Encyclopedia*, Marianne and Jurgen Cieslik discuss the difficulty of actually firing these larger doll heads. Smaller doll heads could be placed on racks and fired without additional support, but larger models required internal support less they collapse; this was, the Encyclopedia states, especially true for socket head models, and in a recent interview, Jurgen Cieslik notes that "the breakage percentage during production must have

The extraordinary way-larger-than-lifesize "Riesenbaby" by Kley and Hahn is shown alongside a 15" Kammer and Reinhardt 115 toddler. Even with bent limb baby body, the Riesenbaby measures a resounding 37". (#70 and 69 in the catalog)

The baby seated is 17" and big sister is a grand 44", or 2 ½ times the size. The size was not only a factor of length, but also of circumference of head, and, further, custom eyes, wigs, even shipping boxes were needed for the grand-sized dolls. Given these additional production expenses, it becomes obvious why the dolls are so rare.

At 34", the size 18 Kestner with closed mouth is 2 ½ times larger than her 15" little friend. (#96 and 97 in this catalog).

The resplendent 40" Steiner bébé even required special glass eyes to accommodate her wire lever mechanism. For size comparison, she is holding a 15" Steiner bébé. (#107 and 108 in the catalog).

Three sizes of Kestner's model 260 are shown side by side to convey size differences. They are 42", 34" and 18" respectively. (#240, 241, and 242 in the catalog)

been terribly high". Too, the larger dolls required greater detail of sculpting that might not be found on smaller dolls; the 1892 registration for a "doll head with eyebrows profiled in the mold" was describing a sculpting detail that all experienced collectors know is distinctively found on large dolls.

Practical matters also contributed to the high cost of the dolls. Consider the shipping costs of a 40" doll. It is not only taller, but also has greater girth, depth, width and weight. Surely, at least four 20" dolls could be shipped in the same space required for one 40" doll. This extra shipping expense would have been passed along to the customer. And the prohibitive import duties by American customs could have contributed to the costs, also. Jurgen Cieslik emphasizes that not enough attention has been paid to the ways in which arbitrary duties influenced the doll market, and it is not unlikely that dolls over a certain size were subject to a duty surcharge.

Size is relative, of course. 18" for a bathing doll, the largest shown here, is extremely rare, particularly given its original swimming play purposes. Few examples of this grand 18" size are known. The others in the comparison photo are 15" and 13". (# 136, 137, 138 in the catalog)

In considering the rarity of grand-sized dolls, collectors would also do well to consider the idea of "large for its type". As an example, a 10" all-bisque doll may not be large, per se, but for its type it certainly is. In that regard, Carol Jean Zvonar's collection, which includes a fine small collection of rare German swimming dolls (known popularly as Frozen Charlotte dolls) offers two models at 18", a size virtually unknown for this genre. This is particularly noteworthy for a style of doll whose size was so significant to its very purposes; the doll must be perfectly proportioned in order to float rather than drown! And it is why larger models are so rarely found.

A fine well-chosen group of large dolls creates a delightful doll environment. While Carole Jean Zvonar chose to exhibit her exceptional collection year-round in playful scenes of childhood, other collectors use them only at holiday times, as did toy stores of yore, creating a delightful "under the Christmas tree" scene. Still others, although lacking the room for a multi-doll collection of grand-sized dolls, add one or two examples as center pieces to their smaller dolls, as a "mannequin" for children's costumes, or simply as a visual perspective. And finally, some collectors who seek only important dolls for their collection, understand the rarity of grand-sized dolls, and choose them for that most classic of reasons "It's wonderful, I've never seen another, and I probably never will again". ❧

A slightly different version of this article appeared in Antique Doll Collector, July 2007 issue.

Index of Doll Makers & Marks

Maker	Mark: *Lot Number*
Schmidt, Bruno	**298**
Schmidt, Franz	**2**
	1271: **296**
	1272: **295**
	1294: **124, 277, 294**
	1295: **1, 89**
Schmitt & Fils	**98, 103**
Schuetmeister & Quendt	251: **121, 122**
Simon & Halbig	**30**
	719: **11**
	939: **10**
	949: **154, 156**
	1029: **123**
	1039: **314**
	1078: **127**
	1079: **128**
	1159: **38, 252**
	1160: **250**
	1248: **6, 8**
	1249: **7**
	1269: **4**
	1279: **5**
	1299: **299**
	1388: **41**
	1398: **42**
Steiner, Jules	**99, 100, 252, 330**
	Series C: **19, 20**
	Figure A: **26, 108, 256, 257**
	Series A: **104**
	Figure C: **107**
Swaine & Co	**139, 140**
Theroude	**28**
Thuillier	**11**
Trautmann	**301**
Vichy	**14, 16, 163, 225**
Wiesenthal	**66, 325**